CONTENTS

PREFACE – BLACK WOMEN IN DANCE: STEPPING OUT OF THE BARRIERS ... 4
PAWLET BROOKES

TIPPING THE BALANCE OF POWER IN THE DANCE WORLD AND BEYOND ... 6
JAWOLE WILLA JO ZOLLAR

THE CONTRIBUTION OF WOMEN IN SUPPORTING THE DANCE OF THE AFRICAN DIASPORA IN BRITAIN ... 22
MERCY NABIRYE

REFLECTION, REVOLUTION AND RESOLUTION: BLACK DANCE IN THE UK 2000 TO 2016 ... 30
DEBORAH BADDOO

THE TALENT IS THERE, THE OPPORTUNITIES ARE NOT ... 38
HILARY S. CARTY

THE DANCE OF LEADERSHIP ... 44
MAUREEN SALMON

INFRASTRUCTURE ... 54
PAM JOHNSON

SEVEN STAGES OF CREATING ... 60
CATHERINE DÉNÉCY

NARRATING SPACES ... 74
ADESOLA AKINLEYE

THE GREY AREA ... 84
JESSICA WALKER

MY DUALITY, MY STRENGTH ... 92
SHARON WATSON

CONTRIBUTORS BIOGRAPHIES ... 100

PREFACE – BLACK WOMEN IN DANCE: STEPPING OUT OF THE BARRIERS
PAWLET BROOKES

The challenge, strength and tenacity of Black women who have struggled for recognition, visibility and the constant reinvention of self in order to dream, be inspired, to take the leap of faith, and to dance, is at the heart of this publication. Their dances, their songs, interpreting old works and other voices, or creating new ones that are unique, proud and ever-evolving, are a major unsung contribution to the evolution of dance today. Black Women in Dance: Stepping out of the Barriers is the fourth in a series of publications that put under the microscope the passion, vision and inspiration of those involved in the world of dance.

The universality of the Black woman is what binds and makes the publication special; the voices are from around the world telling stories of perseverance and vision and the pain and endurance required to become visible in a world full of women but dominated by men and a Eurocentric aesthetic that governs the sector when one thinks dance. The language and technique associated with dance is that of ballet and contemporary. Black Women in Dance introduces a new agenda, that makes room for new voices, new techniques, new styles and pushes the boundaries of races and cultural barriers that hold back creativity allowing Black women to take centre stage and a leadership position in the world of dance.

Names such as Josephine Baker, Pearl Primus, Katherine Dunham, Joan Myers Brown, Jawole Willa Jo Zollar, Judith Jamison, Misty Copeland, L'Antionette Stines, Brenda Edwards and Sharon Watson gained recognition for placing Black women at the heart of dance internationally. They are changing the face of the colonised past introducing hybrid forms, professional classical dance sitting alongside more grounded structured techniques that work with the flexibility and fluidity of the body, marrying strength and grace.

What motivates, drives and inspires artists to bring something new that represents hidden stories, lost voices and a contemporary narrative is touched upon in this publication. Jawole Willa Jo Zollar expresses it as:

"We bring our stories, and our stories are not always present. They are usually under the table or diminished, and we have to have that."

However, there is some comfort that over the last 40 years things have got better and diversity is an integral part of the cultural landscape of the UK. The reality is that when you start to unpack the impact and look more closely at dance, we see there have been some gains but we have also lost a lot. Fewer companies, no summer school, the agencies have merged and technically dancers are perceived as inadequate, unable to cope with the rigour and demands of international choreographers and artistic practice. Maureen Salmon quotes from Bob Marley:

"Time alone, will tell. Think you're in heaven but your living in hell."

These lyrics summed up the sector and the role of Black women, and the primary analysis of the Black Women in Dance, who are under-represented, under-funded and under-acknowledged even when they continue to push the boundaries and do fantastic work.

Black Women in Dance: Stepping out of the Barriers is a missing link in an international story which is not often told from a UK perspective. It makes connections with a number of its sister organisations and artists from across the world who share the same stories, barriers and passion for the sector. It straddles artists and academic considerations in addressing these missing voices and opens up the opportunity for global network and dialogue that is supportive and responsive to the challenges ahead as they sit side-by-side with the commercial world of dance.

Catherine Dénécy writes that the challenges are always there:

"The difference between fine arts, music and dancing is me. My body comes in it, so the whole conversation about race, size, height, the height of your leg, the width of your hips, comes in place. So the Black female body becomes the centre of the conversation sometimes. So for me you have to address that in order to freely dance, you have to come with your body, and accept your body in order to be standing on stage. As it touches the body we are women, I think a whole conversation can start around that. Whereas if I just brought my painting here I would have to deal with who I am. You do what you do because of where you're from and because you know what you are doing. But now it comes from; Where did I go to school? Which were the women I found beautiful? When was I told I was beautiful? All of those things enter the conversation of the Black female body dancing."

This is the challenge of Black Women in Dance and these are the complex range of issues before we begin to talk about technique, this is the untold story of the sector that is brushed aside and this is where the strength has come to reposition the role and place of Black women as they take centre stage from their own perspective.

Pawlet Brookes

Catherine Dénécy, *Guadeloupe, 2013*. Photographer G. Aricique.

TIPPING THE BALANCE OF POWER IN THE DANCE WORLD AND BEYOND

UBW in *Hair Stories*. Photographer Jennifer W. Lester.

JAWOLE WILLA JO ZOLLAR

I can't tell you how excited and thrilled I was to speak at the Black Women in Dance conference, it was such an honour and a return. We toured to Leicester very early in our touring life in 1987 in one of our first tours to Europe. It was such a significant marker for us as a company, so to come back again and be part of this great conference and festival was really fantastic. As a way to give you an introduction to where Urban Bush Women has been and where we are now, I would like to share a video we developed for our 30th anniversary, a transcription of which follows. It's been 31 years now, so it's quite a joy and a pleasure to share this with you.

We started with movement, bodies, shapes, choreography. Then we became a movement, bringing to life untold and untold stories of the disenfranchised, from a woman-centred perspective as members of the African Diaspora community, tipping the balance of power in the dance world and beyond. Our movement made of movement; is fervent and big hearted. We are insistent and active. We are receptive and always learning. We are full of hope. We are Urban Bush Women.

My name is Jawole Willa Jo Zollar and I am the Founding Artistic Director and Chief Visioning Officer of Urban Bush Women. When I formed this company, it was with the philosophy of making work together; dancers, musicians, poets, visual artists. We told stories, beginning with a company of seven women. We were performing all over New York City establishing our voices and right away we were embraced by the women's community, the social arts community, the social justice community. We began touring. We performed 'Anarchy', 'Wild Women' and 'Dinah'; dances about women who made their own way, on their own terms. Our dances had singing and storytelling, and they were bodacious, but during a performance in Charleston, South Carolina, I looked out into the audience and I didn't see any Black people. Well, I saw two. So Urban Bush Women decided to go out and find African American audiences and working class folk, and people of colour, by visiting schools and churches and community centres. Someone told me this was "outreach" hmm… We wanted to go deeper. We made works about homelessness; 'Shelter', and it won awards. 'Lipstick' was about girls becoming women. It showed Urban Bush Women makes work about social justice and the buzz that followed both works led to more touring and more touring led to more outreach. But we still felt we had more to offer.

In the early 1990s we were invited to plan and facilitate a long-term residency in New Orleans. We started calling our work community engagement to distance it from the concept of "outreach". Outreach was a term we began to define as a large institution reaching out but more likely "down" to what it considers a fringe population for the purposes of checking off boxes of how many and where served instead of creating authentic relationships. We entered communities through town hall meetings, and talked to our hosts to let the themes emerge from the community. We didn't present ourselves as experts from New York. We wanted to learn and grow with the communities we were there to serve. And we always kept dance as a powerful centre to the community engagement work. We established our Summer Leadership Institute at Florida State University with a curriculum combining art, culture and social issues and aimed to train a new dancer for a new society. We were going deeper and then in 2000 we faced a financial crisis. It made us look long and hard at what we valued as a company. We fought to survive; we wrote and committed ourselves to core values that still guide us today. Urban Bush Women validates the individual, serves as a catalyst for progressive social change, build and nurtures trust through process, enters communities and co-creates stories, celebrates the African Diaspora, and recognises that place matters.

New works were created and our methodology grew even stronger. We began talking more confidently about our community engagement processes. Then in 2009 I hit a creative wall. With great courage and faith I put the company on a two and a half year hiatus. I wanted us to really look at what we needed to support our artistic work,

Jawole Willa Jo Zollar in Bitter Tongue. Photographer Cylla Von Tiedemann.

our leadership work and our engagement work and the processes that centre that work. We needed to put the art making instead of the market back in the centre. During this time we focused on leadership development, our work through 'BOLD': Builders, Organizers and Leaders through Dance. We reflected on our mission to see where we had drifted. We examined everything. Then we came back strong after taking time to edify and look at that which makes us unique. We deepened our partnership with the People's Institute to strengthen our work, to understand the structural analysis of racism and how it impacts the stories we need to tell.

Research, Do, Delve Deeper, Learn! This exemplifies the Urban Bush Women way. I am, you are, we are Urban Bush Women.

The video gives context and history to the work and now I'm going to go a little into how we articulate where we are now.

ORIGINS OF CURRENT THINKING

I looked back at the idea of post-modernism as a defining place for American modern dance in the 60s and 70s. There was a generative period of experimentation that was mostly defined through a White post-modern lens while ignoring the robust experimentation that was going on in Black and communities of colour.

In looking at the Judson Church, Fluxus, Grand Union and other White postmodernist movements, I began to look at the underlying philosophical frameworks of how people were thinking and creating. At the same time I began examining Black radical experimentation, content, structure and form. I wanted to look at what would be the underlying mechanism that supports Black radical experimentation, and it took me to the 'Ring Shout'. As a person interested in global movements, my primary lens is as an African American woman, raised in segregation who came of age during the Civil Rights and Black Power movements. My international travels have heightened my curiosity and study of what is uniquely American and in particular, African American.

I'm going to offer up a provocative statement.

I'm starting to think that White European derived forms focus on heightened abstraction, form and structure to diminish emotionality. Africanist derived forms focus on heightened emotionality to define form, structure and abstraction. I'm not saying one is better than the other, but I'm saying there are two different ways. However, one has been lifted up as the centre of the universe.

European derived forms are not the centre of the universe; they are part of the universe, but not the centre.

Ballet and classical and contemporary European art forms are part of my training and they have great value. But what if we look at them in the way my dear friend, choreographer Liz Lerman would? She talks about the horizontal in contrast to the vertical and she has a great book called *"Hiking the Horizontal"*. So if we see Hip-Hop, Tap, Ballet, Contemporary Dance, Martha Graham technique and so on… the standards of how we judge what is good, what is excellent, does not hold ballet at the top, or at the centre. And this is a place where, in the United States, there is still a lot of struggle and hierarchy in what gets lifted up as excellent, and what gets funding, and how the many forms of dance are spoken and written about, when ascribing their value.

It's important for us to look at experimentation, and the legacy of experimentation, and creating work in Black radical forms, and I look at everything from music to writing to film, and that was such an important thing to me when coming to Leicester in '87, and seeing the film coming out of the Black community here, and seeing it as a challenge to define and push my own work. As I look at the current landscape, the need for UBW to establish a choreographic centre that lifts up Africanist approaches by female choreographers of colour, particularly in experimental work, is pressing.

UBW's Choreographic Centre is how Urban Bush Women has chosen to go forward to influence our current dance landscape. We launched our Centre in January 2016 with two focuses: supporting and strengthening leadership and vision in individual choreographers, and then bringing about systemic change in the field of dance.

RUNNING TOWARDS THE FIRE WHILE YOU ARE ON FIRE

Another way I describe the aesthetic of the Choreographic Centre is "running towards the fire while you're on fire". That was the urgency in the 60s and 70s that we felt, our communities were on fire, we were on fire and rather than say "no, we're going to go into a different idea and form" and back away from the urgency of the political and social contexts affecting our lives. No! We were saying "we're going to run right into that fire" because we were on fire with passion, anger, frustration, love, joy, and we're going to acknowledge that and create from that. So feeling this urgency to speak truth to power. Bringing the multitude of our traditions to the centre, and looking at the writings that came out, particularly in the 1970s and looking at language, and how language could reflect a whole cultural identity. One example is on language and the value of the vernacular. There was a poet called Don L. Lee, who changed his name to Haki Madhubuti. He wrote a very influential poem at the time, and it took vernacular language and brought the poetry of that language to the surface. One of the lines from the poem is:

"But He Was Cool, or: he even stopped for green lights."

Helping Black female choreographers to find their urgency, their passion and their voice by examining their entire familial, community and cultural history brings a valuing of the many physical and vocal languages that can inform their unique way to tell their story.

THE MARGINS & THE CENTRE – FINDING NEW MODELS BY UNDERSTANDING INTERNALISED RACIAL OPPRESSION

Finding new models, for those of us who have lived involuntarily at the margins – we can find strength from the margins as a way to critique the crumbling centre of White and European dominated culture and ideas, because the centre is changing. It's falling apart and it needs to fall apart. I'm not talking about being marginalised, I'm just saying standing back, we can see what's going on in the centre and we can create from that place and it's a very powerful place.

We can find liberation by examining internalised racial oppression in our methodologies, teaching and art that we produce. So we work with an organisation called the People's Institute for Survival and Beyond, and it does workshops all over the world called understanding and undoing racism. And they hold two central ideas about internalised racial oppression; one is internalised racial superiority and internalised racial inferiority.

Internalised racial superiority is by people who've become to be called White. So it's the assumptions that you learn, you carry, the unexamined assumptions that are a part of that background history, legacy and present day for people who become to be called White.

Internalised racial inferiority is the legacy that we carry as people who've come to be called Black, of how racism, affects us; the unexamined ways the messages of our inferiority are expressed in our art and our life, and how these unexamined manifestations of oppression can show up in our work even with the best of intentions, because when they are unexamined we don't even know it's coming forward. This unconscious, unexamined place is what allows us to duplicate colonised methodologies of creating and teaching dance while de-emphasizing experimentation and risk.

TOWARD A LIBERATORY PRACTICE

In order to create an environment of risk, it means people must have permission to be curious and permission to fail. How many of us grew up with a ballet teacher with a stick? I began to notice that in poor communities and usually in poor communities of colour the most rewarded behaviour is obedience. You see it in the schools. You see it in the institutions. The value that is held up the most is obedience; *obey this step*. I noticed that when I went to institutions of privilege, I saw the highest value and most rewarded behaviour was around critical thinking, not obedience. Obedience is preparing poor people and Black people from the school to prison or military pipeline. But critical thinking is a value that you see in the educational systems populated by those who inhabit race and class privilege. They are prepared to answer the question *"how do you understand the world that you're in and become prepared to comment on and take action in that world"?*

If we're going to step up an environment of risk, we have to embrace critical thinking, curiosity and thinking way outside the lines. I came up in old school teaching methodologies in dance and I have really had to work hard to undo militarism. The old school training process, which meant only the strongest will survive, and the teacher's stance was *"I'm going to let you know if you're one of the weak ones you're going to know real quick, because I'm going to put you down. I'm going to talk about you with your mom and your momma's momma, to make sure that you're strong enough and tough enough"*. I understand this approach and it can be very effective in making an obedient accomplished dancer. There is another way to achieve excellence and grit. You need grit. We need to be tough to move out into the world but not at the expense of our humanity. We can accomplish both. We also need environments where you can think, where you can fail, where you can investigate, where you can inquire, so if our focus is only on obedience then a risk environment doesn't have a chance to succeed.

BLACK WOMEN IN DANCE STEPPING OUT OF THE BARRIERS

UBW in rehearsal for *dark swan*, choreographed by Nora Chipaumire. Photographer Matt Cawrey.

When you jump on a dancer with a correction and you have the force of your authority, you've just cut off risk. If you say *"that's wrong"* and keep repeating that and after a while you get obedience; you might get excellent obedience, but you're not getting the creative, generative dancer that we at Urban Bush Women value and look for. Women and Black women become more victimised by this colonised methodology. Because there are fewer male dancers than women in our field, the male dancer gets a lot of affirmation on the importance of their presence and creative voice. Women are told directly or indirectly you are a dime a dozen. This cuts off the idea that we have an important creative voice.

TEACHING METHODOLOGIES – DECOLONISING OUR METHODOLOGIES

Let's focus on how UBW is looking at decolonising our methodologies as dancers and choreographers as a part of the work of the Choreographic Centre. When we started this Choreographic Centre the idea was to bring about a different awareness, understanding and examination of our practice as a way to create liberation methodologies. This idea of decolonising our methodologies and how we train in dance is essential. Dance traditionally has been hierarchical, that there's an all knowing teacher, that by hook or by crook gets you to submit to the authority of that teacher, and participant or student then regurgitates back through the form the teacher has given what they have learned.

There's another way. There's another possibility. We hold that the generative dancer, holistic dance training and choreographic practice follow UBW's process of art making which involves iterative cycles of rigorous embodied research informed by a vast field of movement practices and by radical Black experimentation in the fields of culture, politics and history. The UBW performers develop a self-directed solo practice that allows them to devise original works through a collaborative process.

The dancer becomes responsible for that research and in doing so helps the dance gain a sense of their own power. It is not enough to know a step, to be able to execute steps. There is a complex training methodology that supports our work that includes ballet, modernist and post-modern forms, contemporary, vernacular and social dance as well as theatre based practices. There is a heavy somatics focus that is a part of our work and training, and it includes the Ring Shout: ways of knowing that are ancestral, that are connected to our elders in our community, and at its core is pelvic awareness.

UBW in rehearsal for *dark swan*, choreographed by Nora Chipaumire. Photographer Matt Cawrey.

When I teach at the university (I teach at Florida State University) most of the dancers who have come into the programme are primarily ballet trained or coming from a background in dance competition. So pelvic awareness is a big thing, because they have been taught to stabilise their pelvis and hold onto that stabilisation for dear life. We're saying that even within certain modern practices, that's a holding, tensing pattern that does not allow you to be responsive. A question that guides our research is *"how can we create core strength and core stability without that holding, tensing pattern within the pelvis"?* How do we honour our Africanist traditions of movement practice that release and see the fluidity in the whole spine? Both things can be true, it's not an either or. It's a di-unital concept, both things can be true – core stability and pelvic fluidity. We're looking at connectivity, not only physically, spatially, but also historically, politically. When we're working for connection, initiation and sequencing, all of that connects to history, political awareness. We're saying these are connected, and we bring this into the room by our assumptions whether we've examined them or not.

We look at strength and strength is very important to us. As a person who grew up with a certain desire to understand and be a part of what people called the *"release"* movement, I found that the many ways I wanted to express strength, I wanted to express power and I wanted to express *"grit"* and resilience with Africanist movement practices at the core were not reflected in what people at that time were calling *"release"*. But I needed to express strength, power and grit because that is part of our cultural lineage. I want risk, inquiry, investigation and experimentation inside of a training methodology that would help me gain a full sense of my power and my full humanity.

UBW'S CHOREOGRAPHIC CENTRE

Our Choreographic Centre and our work with choreographers support the development of leadership and the strengthening and supporting the vision of Black female choreographers and women of colour choreographers.

I like to use nature as a way to bring clarity to conceptual ideas. We have a structure of three cohorts of choreographic development each with a different need.

THE SWAMP AND THE DESERT – COHORT ONE – FINDING AND ARTICULATING VOICE

What I see in the U.S. is a pattern of disempowerment around subject matter and choreographic choices. When a young, Black, choreographer is starting, they are usually starting from the swamp, the gut, the feeling. It's often in response to something that has happened. In Florida and across the U.S. we saw lots of pieces responding to the murder of a young man, Trayvon Martin. We saw lots of work like that responded to with rage – from the gut. Often the works are emotional, unsophisticated and didactic. I see this as a beginning step in their choreographic journey. In the universities I see they are often cut off at the limb with an unwillingness to see the validity of the choreographer's ideas. I hear *"that's bad work"*. As opposed to saying that is the beginning, this is a beginning place working from the swamp, and this is an important place. If we can value that as an important place then we can learn how to put the tools in place to help them make this work better. What I often see in the very budding voice is a lack of support for the choreographer. The choreographer gets very confused, disempowered and starts to then take on *"if I want to be a good choreographer I need to leave behind my culture, my passions and take on other kinds of assumptions"*. I see working from the swamp as a first and important step.

At some point we have to go to the desert, that means you have to strip away, you have to take away all of the essentials. You have to be in this kind of barren, vulnerable place that's very scary. But it's really not barren, because there's lots of life in the desert, you don't necessarily see it at first. This process with the swamp and the desert is what we are identifying as our Cohort One – the emerging choreographer. We are examining how we support emerging choreographers, looking at their work from the swamp, and then being in a process of the desert, helping them strip away assumptions. It's not an audience centric process, and this is where I find that audiences that have been programmed to only see the values of *"steps"*, have very little patience for this stage of investigation, because it's experimental and it doesn't quite know where it's going. We can educate audiences to be curious and excited and watching work in this developmental stage. Yet, I see experimental White choreographers critiqued in a very different way in the US, when I see White experimental choreographers who are in the desert, who are stripping away, but who are less concerned with social political issues and more concerned with form, structure and abstraction. This in itself is not the problem. What is the problem is the valuing of one type of beginning experimentation over the other.

In both of these cases it's not audience centric, but the audience is important as a witness. The audience is not at the centre of what the choreographer needs to learn. So when Urban Bush Women first started, my training was Cunningham, Graham, Limón, and that was their voices. I wanted to find my voice, to strip down. I went to the UBW dancers, and declared you cannot point your feet, I don't want you to *"pull up"*, I want us to go to a primal, emotional place. Strip away everything that we've thought about in order to find a unique voice. It's a very important period, and it must be supported. The choreographer has to be encouraged to wildly experiment and strip away fear based on assumptions of what *"good choreography"* is supposed to look like.

THE MOUNTAINS – COHORT TWO – ARTICULATING AND DEEPENING CRAFT, RIGOUR AND VISION

Then what we have is our second cohort. People who are learning to scale the mountains. You need engineering and tools. You need craft. You can't just go up the mountain and hope for the best, you've got to figure out the ways in which you're going to get up and down that mountain. This is where your craft and your rigour, and your attention to detail come in. You've got to have a strong rope and you've got to have tested your systems. You need support to achieve your highest vision. In regard to our middle cohort of choreographers, this is where we want to assist. This is where dramaturgy comes in really strong; why are you doing, what are you doing? Really being granular looking at the processes of the work. If we do this with the first cohort, it's almost too soon; it's almost shutting it off. We want to turn on the valve for that Cohort One. For Cohort Two we want to support how the vision climbs to the highest peaks. How can you create your most excellent work, and how can we support that? And we're putting together teams of dramaturgs, historians, directors, choreographers who can mentor this process.

THE OCEAN AND THE ISLAND – COHORT THREE – SUSTAINING THE VISION

Now for Cohort Three, you are doing your work but you are in the middle of the ocean. You have vast possibilities. You are getting support, commissions and residencies but you need a lifeboat because you don't have infrastructure. You don't have the things that support this amazing vision. In our performance you will see the work of Nora Chipaumire's vision with *dark swan*. So how can we at the Choreographic Centre support that period of being in the ocean, where the possibilities are vast and unlimited but you can swim out there by yourself forever.

THE FOREST

Then somewhere when you're in that third cohort you get lost in the forest. So you start to achieve success, build infrastructure and an organisation to support your vision and everyone's telling you that you're doing good work but you've lost your path because you start to think *"maybe success means this"* or *"maybe success means that"* or *"I should keep doing that. That was successful, maybe I should repeat that."* So you start to get lost in the forest and begin to second guess your path or maybe you can't find your path anymore

THE ISLAND

Then you go to an island. Spend some time on the island, reflect, come back into self.

Then actually you start this process all over again. These are the three cohorts, but anyone of them can get lost in the forest at any time, any one of them might need to go to the desert to strip away. Any one of them might need tools to scale a mountain. So this is what our hope is to do in terms of supporting choreographers. So when people ask us what the structure around the Choreographic Centre is, where it's housed, we answer that it's not housed in a building. In fact we actually don't want a building, unless it comes with millions and millions of money for capital to operate the building, because we're seen too many organisations go under from having a building they can't maintain. When we get to that point when we can have that, yes we want a building, we want a space, but part of that we want to focus on now is partnerships with organisations that have spaces; University centres, community centres that can provide residencies, that can provide support for the work that we want to do.

The Choreographic Centre is an amoeba-like structure. It is responsive. We're not saying the Choreographic Centre is rigid. We're flexible and responsive. As creative people we're always changing. We need to change.

This is our greatest challenge with funders. They want to define, hard and fast ways in which we're working. And what we've learned also from our Summer Leadership Institute, which I'll also talk about, is that from our community practice it is the same. Funders would say *"what are you going to go out and do in the community, outline it and tell us your outcomes"*. If we tell you that we haven't done our process, our process is to go and talk with a community, seek a mutual agreement, look at mutual risk, look at mutual investment and then we can talk about what might happen. But if we write down what will happen in advance, we've not been in process, we've been in the funders' process, not our process. So the same way with the Choreographic Centre, how do we explain this? We want the funders to understand that this process is important because it is the process we use in creating work. How many people have written a description for a grant for funding for a piece that you haven't even been in the studio to discover what's real yet? You're trying to write a good fiction, but the truth is you really don't know because you haven't been there yet, but you try and make up the best fiction that you can in order to secure the funds. What if funders really understood that?

UBW'S SUMMER LEADERSHIP INSTITUTE (SLI) AS THE RESEARCH BODY FOR THE CHOREOGRAPHIC CENTRE.

Going back into our SLI, which is now in its 16th year. The SLI looks at activism and art making, again in a holistic way. Now doing it 16 times, not 16 times in a row, but 16 times, we started being a four-week SLI, but we realised we only got young people, because they take off four weeks in the summer. Moving it to be a 10-day allowed a more diverse group of participants.

So this is what we've learned from Urban Bush Women's SLI, and what we hope to embody in our Choreographic Centre. Lizzy Cooper Davis, has summed up UBW's work and belief system with the following statements:

1. WE BELIEVE COMMUNITY IS STRENGTHENED BY EACH INDIVIDUAL'S FULL PRESENCE AND HOLISTIC ENGAGEMENT.

We want to bring all of our histories forward; personal biography, presence of mind, body and spirit. We're not saying one history is more important than the other, but how do we create an environment where *everybody* feels they can bring their history forward?

2. WE BELIEVE THAT ART ARTICULATES COMMUNITIES, AESTHETICS AND ETHICS.

When I talk about the Ring Shout, you see the Ring Shout from Beyoncé to our dearly beloved Prince, you see those forms within Black American traditions. You see it in Arthur Mitchell's work, you see and hear it all over the world.

3. WE EMBRACE MULTIPLE ROLES: TEACHER, STUDENT, ORGANISER, LEADER, MENTOR, MENTEE, ELDER, ETC.

There is not a hierarchy of what that is; it's a role at a particular point in time. If I only say I am a mentor, I am an elder; I lose an opportunity to learn and to grow. These roles can happen all at the same time, you might be all of them at once.

4. WE VALUE EMBODIED LEARNING AND MOVEMENT AS METAPHORS FROM MOVEMENT BUILDING.

When we're learning about racism in our SLI we also look at it's physicality; how it's impacting us and where is this information hitting us? And we look at how we can then embody our internal states to learn more about who we are and how we are processing information.

5. WE STRESS THE IMPORTANCE OF AFFIRMATION, HONOURING & CELEBRATION.

When I was growing up in Kansas City, we use to have a party for everything. So your dog got house trained, you have a party, because it's important to celebrate. It's a tradition. We do hard work so we have to affirm and celebrate what we've accomplished. Sometimes they're big accomplishments, and sometimes they're small, but that tradition of honouring and celebrating is an important part of communities from the African Diaspora. I grew up in segregation in Kansas City, Missouri, so I didn't encounter White people socially until I was in college. When I was invited to a party by a group of White friends I kept sitting there thinking when is the dancing going to start? A couple of hours now, lots of drinking but when are we going to start dancing? Because in the tradition I grew up in, a party was a celebration of dance. Somebody said you were invited to a party it meant a celebration of dancing, not a celebration of drinking and talking. So these cultural distances, of affirmation through dancing, this is what we're saying is important to us as a cultural value.

BLACK WOMEN IN DANCE STEPPING OUT OF THE BARRIERS 17

Walking with 'Trane, Chapter 2. Photographer Rick McCollough.

6. WE RECOGNISE THAT WISDOM RESIDES IN THE GROUP AND MODEL LEADERSHIP THROUGH FACILITATED DIALOGUE AND COLLABORATION RATHER THAN INSTRUCTION

The dialogue and collaboration with the dancers and their research that they are bringing to the table is very important to how work is created, how we're learning. If I am in a dialogue with myself, then it gets convoluted in my head. I've got to know from other people, and I don't ever believe that I'm the smartest person in the room. I think that's a real trap.

7. WE VALUE THE PROCESS OF CONTINUED RISK, FALL AND RECOVERY OVER ASSERTIONS OF STABILITY, BELIEVE THE WOBBLING IS THE BALANCING AND THAT BEING PUSHED OFF BALANCE WILL ENHANCE RATHER THAN INHIBIT THE GROUP'S ABILITY TO PERFORM AND SUCCEED.

I grew up with that concept, *"be on your leg"* and that holding, gripping, pattern to get on the leg does not create stability. The oscillation and the movement that you have to find, that you have to be aware of in order to find stability is really important, and sometimes it's big, and sometimes it's really tiny. So that the wobbling and being pushed off balance, deliberate destabilisation, within the learning process, a place where you are destabilised in order to learn. It doesn't mean someone holding a stick over you and beating you into submission, but it means by unearthing assumptions of what you hold to be real. If this is what I have known, in order to find a new place, I'm going to have to let go of something. That is going to be destabilising. It's going to change something, shake up something and destabilise my whole emotional self, and if I'm not willing to go through that whole destabilisation I will only do what I know, I will default back to what is comfortable. We talk about this in the company all the time, be aware of your defaults, because they lead you back to what's comfortable.

We've got to be willing to risk, be off balance, and to understand that that is what's going to take us to a new place, that is what is going to help us succeed and find new information. What's true one year is not true the next year and I can definitely tell you that from the ageing process. What's true one year, one month, is not true the next. It's a constant realigning of oneself and one's environment.

THE RING SHOUT – THE BIRTH OF BLACK AMERICAN ART MAKING TRADITIONS

The Ring Shout is a particular Black American form. When I look at how experimentation and dance in the Black community is shaped, the Ring Shout is the foundation for the practice. The following statements are articulated by Lizzy Cooper Davis in her documentation of UBW's Summer Leadership Institute work.

- *The Ring Shout is a practice that originated in the Caribbean and US south, and was an embodied practice of worship of the enslaved.*

- *Participants moved in a counter-clockwise circle while singing songs of worship or prayer to the rhythms of their shuffling feet and clapping hands. The ring facilitated the range of deep expression and release essential for the health and maintenance of the community*

- *Sterling Stuckey (1988) explains, the Ring Shout was "a central organising principle of slave culture"*

In the United States, what was really interesting about how slavery was practiced is that the enslaved were separated from each other – ethnic groups were deliberately divided – there was a conscious movement to make sure that ethnic groups were not together and could not speak the same languages. As the practice of Christianity was imposed or brought to the enslaved, the slave owners were disturbed by the movements with which the African American people brought to their worship. We didn't just sit still and sing, as was the Anglican practice. The African enslaved were moving and embodying their worship traditions. This started to become embodied into the Ring Shout. The rhythms of the Ring Shout are achieved through clapping hands and the use of a broomstick in replacement for the drum. This was due to the fact that drums were outlawed very early on during the period of slavery – beginning approximately in 1740 and continuing forward. The shuffling feet, the hands, the clapping, the broom or stick that's pounded on the floor; those became another way of the drum being expressed. The ring shout is the way we released and expressed our feelings and ways of creating community survival and resilience. Davis further elaborates:

"During a time when their dancing was forbidden and considered blasphemous in religious settings, the Ring Shout's subtle footwork fell strategically outside European definitions of dance and thus smuggled the movement so integral to African cosmologies into Black American prayer. Within the safety of the ring, expression ranged from supplication to joy and from flailing grief to trance-like prayer but the circle, its motion and its song, remained constant."

Hearing about the shout and experiencing it are two different things, at the conference I thought it would be interesting to share a bit of the Ring Shout with the company, the transcription of which follows.

There are a lot of different Ring Shout songs. In the shout there's a caller, clappers or broom person and singers. It's a call and response form.

Tendayi sings: I say *"run Mary run!"* and you say *"oh lord!"*

Tendayi: *"Run Martha Run!"*

Group responds: *"Oh Lord!"*

Tendayi: *"Run Mary Run!"*

Group: *"Oh Lord!"*

Tendayi: *"You got the right to the tree of life! You got a right, you got a right!"*

Group: *"You got the right to the tree of life!"*

Tendayi: *"You got a right, you got a right!"*

Group: *"You got the right to the tree of life!"*

And there's the clapping and you can join us in the clapping, and you can create sounds with the clapping. So if you go to the base clap you want to cup [your hands]. Higher pitched clapping [with your fingers] and mid-level [flat hands]. You can choose where you want to come in – if you want to be in the bass, the soprano. And when I ask them to move, they're young, they're dancers – so I ask them to think how their grandmothers would have moved, otherwise we can go into a more contemporary idea. There are people in the US who are beautifully taking the legacy of the Ring Shout into contemporary forms. I want to give you more of a sense of its legacy. The idea is really to embody that place of grandmothers, grandfathers, great-grandmother, great-grandfathers – our ancestors.

Many of you may recognise aspects of the shout in the masterful work of Mr Ailey, 'Revelations'. You may also see the actions of the shout embodied through caricature and humour. I think of it as a sacred dance. It is sacred dance; it carries sacred histories and contains sacred practices. In contemporary practice you'll see the legs crossed, you'll see, we talk about shouting churches or Holy Ghost churches, or Pentecostal churches, and you may have seen people in the various aspects of the shout. We recognise that it is a somatic process, practice and belief. It is about connecting an internal state to an external state and it is rooted in all aspects of African American culture.

If we think of the Ring Shout as foundational to the Black experience in worship, prayer, music and movement, we can begin to see how many historical and contemporary forms have their roots in the Ring Shout and the importance of this legacy to what differentiates the art-making, storytelling and physical impulses from the origins of the White post-modern experimentation and art-making. Black being-ness is rooted in this tradition and continues to shape what we hold important to bringing our art to the world.

WE CREATE THE CONTAINER AND BELIEVE THE CIRCLE WILL HOLD US, HONOURING THE ETHICS OF COMMUNITY INHERENT IN THE RING SHOUT.

Within the value of the Ring Shout, if we create an environment where we can *Be*, where we know we are supported by a community, it doesn't mean everything's lovely, it means that we're challenged, that there's rigour. Then we are honouring the ethics of the Ring Shout, which honours the struggles we go through at the same time as moving forward toward resolution.

In the spirit of learning, generosity, love and gratitude, I'm so happy that we have been in Leicester, that we have been able to share something about Urban Bush Women's journey, how we're thinking right now, and where we hope to go.

REFERENCES

UBW 30th Anniversary Video, https://vimeo.com/149164982

Stuckey, Sterling (1988) *Slave Culture: Nationalist Theory and the Foundations of Black America.* Oxford University Press

BLACK WOMEN IN DANCE STEPPING OUT OF THE BARRIERS 21

UBW in *I Don't Know, But I've Been Told, If You Keep on Dancin', You Never Grow Old.* Photographer Cylla von Tiedemann.

22 · BLACK WOMEN IN DANCE STEPPING OUT OF THE BARRIERS

THE CONTRIBUTION OF WOMEN IN SUPPORTING THE DANCE OF THE AFRICAN DIASPORA IN BRITAIN

Bullies Ballerinas Dance Company dancing at Interchange Studios 24, March 1995. Choreography by Pearl Jordan & Jeanefer Jean Charles. Photographer Dee Conway. © Lebrecht Music & Arts

MERCY NABIRYE

On 1 April 2016 The Association of Dance of the African Diaspora (ADAD) officially merged with Dance UK, Youth Dance England and National Dance Teachers Association to form a new UK body for Dance 'One Dance UK'. The aim is to have a strong and unified voice which represents specialism areas including, children and young people, industry professionals, dance artists and practitioners, dance teachers, academics, dance of the African Diaspora practice and a focus on the healthier dancer. My role in One Dance UK is to lead the specialism area of Dance for the African Diaspora (DAD). The Association of Dance of the African Diaspora (ADAD) was established in 1994 and was for the most part of its twenty-one years of existence the main support organisation for Black dancers and those who work with dance forms of Africa and African Diaspora-origin. Soon after its twenty first birthday it merged with One Dance UK. Its projects will continue under this new organisation. At the time of writing the merger that has produced One Dance UK is barely five months old.

In this paper I will highlight the role of women in supporting the Dance of the African Diaspora in Britain through discussing the part women have played in bringing ADAD to this point. It is interesting to note that every chair and leader, co-ordinator, manager or director of ADAD has been female. Though ADAD has also had male board members, women have always been at the helm. Interestingly enough ADAD has never run any women-specific or women-only projects. It was formed to support both men and women. So in looking at the contribution of women to ADAD I am looking at what style of leadership and kind of the projects the organisation produced over the years and what we can learn from this. ADAD was a dance support organisation which had a function of creating and developing the subsidised context so that it was more supportive of Black dancers or those working with dance forms from Africa and the Diaspora. First I will discuss the importance of support organisations to dance in general and Dance of the African Diaspora in particular. At the end of my paper I will reflect on how the support of Dance of the African Diaspora will continue under One Dance UK.

THE IMPORTANCE OF DANCE SUPPORT ORGANISATIONS

Dance as a profession requires the intervention of support organisations. Most dancers are independent artists and work outside company structures. The world of work for dance constantly changes, impacted by policies from social, cultural, political and educational trends and settings of the time. Audiences for new styles of dance have to be developed. They do not simply appear. Support organisations help dancers navigate changes in workplace as well as issues around creativity. Changes in policy and funding can be even more complicated for those working in Dance of the African Diaspora. This is because of social policy around inclusion or issues to do with race or simply because there might be less research and information on their dance practice. This means there are fewer 'tool-kits' available that the dancer can use to adapt their work to a new context, for example develop a curriculum for their work in higher education or a proposal that enables them to work in health. This is evident in the research on the sector. I will quote from two reports. The first is 'Time for Change' (2000) written by Hermin McIntosh, Lorraine Yates and Claudette McDonald. The second is a preliminary research report 'ADAD in the North' which was prepared by Ida Hanni Brandt. Through their finding both reports reflect the importance of having an organisation intervene and develop and sustain a professional context for dance.

'Time for Change' shows that issues threatening the professional dancer's career are often of an institutional nature, outside the dancer's control. On page 43, *Section 3: Issues arising from the findings 1.1* it reads:

"From a series of ...interviews it was clear that the range of issues thrown up were often well beyond the sole domain of the cultural sector. Many of the issues were about the wider social, political and economic exclusion of such groups from the mainstream of societies' institutions. Issues broadly included the inability to gain access into the mainstream cultural platforms, invisibility of any significant awards to black organisations, black communities not gaining access to developmental resources. There was a need to have greater involvement across the board of ethnic minorities in the total cultural fabric of society".

The report in other words is arguing that some of the issues that impact on the dance profession for Black dance go beyond the cultural sector and requires the intervention at an institutional level. In the early years of ADAD its choreographic platforms provided opportunities for certain producers from mainstream organisations to engage with emerging choreographers from African and Caribbean backgrounds. It was through the roadshows that took Black dancers into schools that some teachers began to see the relevance of their work for young people. The platform and the roadshow created an institutional bridge.

Ida Hanni Brandt's report 'ADAD in North' (2009) demonstrates the same point. In writing the report Ida asked members of the dance community (i.e. Yorkshire, the North-West and the North-East of England), to give their perspectives on how ADAD might be able to contribute to addressing current dance development needs in their regions. Representatives for the local Arts Council England (North-West, North-East, and Yorkshire); the national and regional dance agencies; independent dance artists and dance companies in the region and academic dance scholars, were approached in order to obtain a diverse sample of perspectives on issues in the regions pertaining to the work ADAD was already engaging in on the national level. The report summarises current concerns for development needs of Black dance artists and artists practising dance of the African Diaspora; and gives suggestions for ADAD's future work in the region. One of the strongest messages coming through during the research was that ADAD could bring a specialised perspective, but would seek to work in collaboration with the dance agencies, companies, and independent artists that are present in the regions. The suggested focus points and areas to work on were categorised as Network and Support, Education and Inspiration, Creating Opportunities, Focusing on the Local, Debate and Research. To quote a few respondents:

"The 'breaking' community in Leeds don't come near official agencies and funding bodies – they would rather go off and do their own thing"

"ADAD could provide an alternative for artists that don't feel at home here [with national dance agencies currently present]"

"Individual artists like me really need a contact which also offers mental support and listens to you and believes in you and your experiences"

"We need to know the British history to create inspiration for young emerging artists"

"There is currently only one dance agency in the NW that has a dedicated Community Dance Artist for African Peoples' Dance"

"Having the ADAD perspective there in the region might help to improve the inclusion of artists who do not go the conventional vocational route or get a university degree"

"The realisation of potential regional, national, and international debates have yet to be realised through presenting the artists with a focal contact and networking point in an ADAD officer who is present in the region".

The report contributed to ADAD opening a hub in the North which enabled it to provide some of the needed support.

Historically women leaders have led on the development of this kind of support in dance as demonstrated by the history of ADAD. Creating partnerships is central to support the work. Partnerships create opportunities, opportunities which dancers can take advantage of as independent workers. Supporting dance as a profession requires leaders who can identify what skills dancers need to learn, be these creative skills or business skills, and seek ways of providing this training or finding partners who might supply this training. Supporting Dance of the African Diaspora also includes promoting the dance forms and aesthetics which underpin choreographic practices. The leaders of ADAD contributed in two ways – developing a sustainable infrastructure and by developing the practice.

A SHORT HISTORY OF ADAD

ADAD was setup in 1994. Quoting 'Funmi Adewole in the recent ADAD 21st Anniversary edition of HOTFOOT,

'..Marie McCluskey MBE was one of the main drivers behind the establishment of ADAD. She was approached by some concerned practitioners to help set up a forum to support their work. ADAD was formed as a practitioner led organisation driven by its steering committee of artists and coordinated by an administrator. The first was June Gamble, followed by Deborah Baddoo. When ADAD was first established it concentrated on raising the profile of Black dancers.....who were looking to explore new ways of working that did not fit in with the mainstream aesthetics and looking to establish their own companies. The ADAD newsletter was established …. It made the context for the performance of work that had an African, Caribbean or Black aesthetic tangible'.

Denise Rowe, ADAD Trailblazer Champion, *'She who walks'* showcase at The Place, 2014. Photographer Foteini Christofilopoulou.

She also notes that ADAD presented performance platforms accompanied by a road show, as well as forums for sharing ideas, information and debate. The projects ADAD organised gave a platform to a number of dancers making larger organisations aware of them and giving them opportunities to create work which prepared the way for some to become choreographers running their own companies at a later stage. 'Funmi attributes to the efficacy of ADAD at that point to the experience of its first co-ordinators June Gamble and Deborah Baddoo who devised projects of bridging the gaps between larger, mainstream organisations and Black dancers.

When the practitioner-led model began to falter as artists' careers expanded, Sheron Wray stepped in to lead the organisation with Debbie Thomas as development manager. Sheron invited key practitioners including 'Funmi Adewole, Judith Palmer, Kwesi Johnson, Robert Hylton and Alicia Ciciani to join the steering committee. She used her network both with other dancers and with organisations to stop the organisation from closing and give it a new lease of life. Not long after this ADAD led by 'Funmi Adewole negotiated with Jeanette Siddall, then Director of Dance UK to enter into a strategic alliance. This gave funders the confidence that ADAD would be able to deliver its projects. This also enabled ADAD to receive organisational development funds. The strategic alliance between ADAD and Dance UK when established in June 2003 was to serve as a form of organisational development for ADAD and a means for Dance UK to develop its cultural diversity agenda. 'Funmi as programme manager carried out a range of projects to help decide the direction the organisation should take, under the mentorship of Jeanette Siddall. It was during this period that the steering committee decided that the organisation needed a new way of working and to develop a strategy to keep it sustainable – the organisation focussed on critical discourse. ADAD hoped to re-emerge as an independent organisation to help facilitate a stronger infrastructure for the dance forms of the African Diaspora, raise the level of discourse around the work, and through collaborative initiatives create professional development opportunities for dancers.

The flagship programmes today took shape during the alliance. They include the Trailblazers Professional Development Fellowship programme which offers bursaries and a tailored mentoring programme to artists with creative spark, ambition and leadership potential was initiated in 2003, the Hotfoot magazine which became an online journal in 2005 and The Heritage project – a photographic exhibition 'Black Dance in Britain: 1930s to 1990s – Moments', which is accompanied by a reader 'Voicing Black Dance: The British experience 1930s to 1990s'. Pamela Zigomo implemented the Heritage project whilst 'Funmi returned as chair. She produced a launch event at the now defunct Theatre Museum, saw to the publication of the reader, organised a year of workshops. Pamela's ingenious marketing skills enabled her to raise the profile of the organisations.

When ADAD exited the strategic alliance in 2011 it became an independent registered charity governed by a board of trustees and a director, Jeanette Bain-Burnett. She took over the reins from Pamela Zigomo whilst Caroline Hinds replaced 'Funmi Adewole as Chair. Under Jeanette ADAD created the Bloom festival which started as a day event in at the South Bank in 2009. The Re:generations International conference, UK's only gathering which brings together dance artists, scholars and managers to discuss international perspectives intending to shape future practice in Dance of the African Diaspora, was set up in 2010. A hub was set up in Leeds in the North managed by a coordinator. A programmer in the South West region was recruited soon after. Activity in the regions was enhanced by the securing Arts Council England 3 year funding and National Portfolio status. For Dance UK, working with ADAD provided a culturally diverse profile, culturally diverse members, improved sector credibility, expertise in African People's Dance and the Black dance sector.

In taking over the role of director from Jeanette in 2012 I focused on developing the Bloom Festival into a national event, creating partnerships with organisations around the country. I also extended ADAD's international partnerships, creating links with the organisation in Canada, in America, Germany and East Africa. As director of the organisation, I appreciated the passion and genuine support I got from the board members chaired by Judith Palmer, who enabled me to successfully execute and raise the standard of the flagship programmes we have to date. I identified and kept close to key people who have tirelessly driven the agenda for Dance of the African Diaspora for a number of decades and in various ways. I have had rich conversations and these have informed my understanding of the practice as it was back then and I have used my learning as a baseline when making strategic decisions for current practice and to support emerging and future leaders in dance in all its diverseness. ADAD has been keen to give honour where honour is due. For this reason Judith Palmer initiated the ADAD Lifetime achievement award honouring the outstanding contribution made by individuals to the practice and appreciation of African Diaspora dance in the UK and beyond. Beverley Glean is the first woman to be awarded the ADAD Lifetime Achievement Award in March 2016. She set up IRIE! dance theatre in 1985 and a Foundation degree course for African People's Dance which is currently the only university validated course of its kind in the UK to date. Other women who have influenced the practice within the African Diaspora, who I keep on my radar, include Greta Mendez, who was co-director of the first funded Black dance touring company in the UK, The MAAS Movers and Dollie Henry who has contributed to Jazz practice for a significant time, to name but a few and the list goes on.

THE LEGACY OF FEMALE LEADERSHIP WITHIN DANCE OF THE AFRICAN DIASPORA

This short history shows the ability of women leaders to build bridges and partnerships and our willingness to share information with each other and negotiate terrains that enabled us to keep going even when the organisation struggled financially. The legacy of female leadership in ADAD is arguably their methods of supporting dance. Investing in initiatives that might seem intangible such as critical discourse, raising the profile of artists, forming partnerships and sharing information have been something which ADAD's leaders have done. This thinking shaped the projects that it delivered. If we think about it – the focus has been on context rather than star individuals. Over the twenty-one years ADAD has produced choreographic platforms, roadshows, newsletters and magazines both paper-based and online, books, a photo exhibition, a heritage project, communication days, workshops, conferences and dance festivals.

Even the Trailblazers professional development fellowship programme is about the context of dance. Since 2003 ADAD has cultivated excellence and leadership in dance, supporting some 38 fellows. Of these, 26 are women. The trailblazers is not a women-specific programme. It acknowledges leadership in all facets of the profession. It supports dance researchers, teachers, writers, producers. Trailblazers have gone on to nurture others and take centre stage in the creative industries. These include champion trailblazers Vicki Igbokwe, Alesandra Seutin, Adesola Akinleye, Ithalia Forel and Denise Rowe. Profiles of all 38 trailblazers can be found on www.onedanceuk.org. It supports people who inspire and who enable dance to exist as work.

We can take from the history of ADAD some ideas about how we can develop our dance companies and dance careers. Dance artists could form collectives and support each other's work, lobby organisations for specific kinds of infrastructure support. The emergence of One Dance UK suggests that partnerships are the sustainable way to work.

THE MERGER – ONE DANCE UK

Caroline Miller's report in 2010 outlines that the major budget cuts necessitated the Arts Council and the Department of Culture Media and Sport (DCMS) to prioritise partnership working, alliances and mergers. She goes on to state that since 2010, the way dance artists work and manage their careers is very different from the environment and career paths of dance artists in the 1980s when most dance support organisations were formed. There are cross overs in the services the support organisations are providing. With less money available from funders and from dance professionals there was a question of whether there was a way that support organisations could form a federation that would be the official governing body for the dance sector – effectively giving dancers at all stages of their careers a one-stop-shop support organisation – encouraging knowledge exchange, sharing back end costs, and counter acting the repeated claim from government and other outside organisations that they find the dance sector confusing because there isn't a single body representing dance that they can deal with.

'The Art of Partnering' report produced by Kings College London in 2016 states:

'In conclusion we see a number of recurring themes that are driving partnership policy in the subsidised cultural sector. These pertain to the following factors

-maximising the impact of modest investment;

-developing interesting and innovative cultural products; and

-reaching wider audiences

All of this is driven by a desire to be rational – to recognise that the objective of broad national policy can only be reached with the coordination of fragmented and dispersed resources. It seems that while there are complexity and scarce resources there will be the need for partnership. Neither of these processes look like slowing down and partnership will continue to be part of the policy toolkit for the foreseeable future'.

The aim of One Dance UK is to contribute to creating effective management infrastructures to support artists and small arts organisations with their business and professional development in order for them to be sustainable without compromising on creativity. One Dance UK will be a contribution to attempts to generate a deeper understanding of the complexities that make effective partnering. There is a commitment to bridge boundaries in a principled and effective way to address a common purpose to think differently and be more ambitious, learning from each other, developing and delivering projects together. Below are a list of projects initiated by ADAD that now exist under One Dance UK:

- The Trailblazers Professional Development Fellowship programme which offers bursaries and a tailored mentoring programme to artists with creative spark, ambition and leadership potential was initiated in 2003. A second strand followed in 2011 aimed at past recipients who had demonstrated strong leadership and entrepreneurial spirit. To date there are 36 trailblazers on the alumni who are key leaders in the sector.

- The Open Stage choreographic platform for work in progress was initiated with venue partners in 2008.

- Hotfoot Magazine reverted to being an online magazine in 2005 and is currently an invaluable resource for research and documenting the practice in the African Diasporas.

- The Heritage project – a photographic exhibition 'Black Dance in Britain: 1930s to 1990s – Moments', which is accompanied by a reader 'Voicing Black Dance: The British experience 1930s to 1990s' was initiated in 2007 as a national touring exhibition which aims to make a distinctive contribution to collecting, conserving, interpreting and narrating history and heritage that informs the work of Black Dancers in contemporary Britain. Since its launch it has been viewed by a footfall of over 60,000 people.

- The Bloom National Festival, a celebration of dance of the African Diaspora at several venues and spaces showcasing artists to thousands of audiences up and down the country for several months, started as a day event at the South Bank in 2009.

- Re:generations International conference, a UK gathering which brings together dance artists, scholars and managers to discuss international perspectives intending to shape future practice in Dance of the African Diaspora, was set up in 2010.

- ADAD Lifetime Achievement Award to honour contribution to dance of the African Diaspora in the UK.

Whilst celebrating ADAD's legacy, we should acknowledge that the achievements to date since ADADs inception in 1994 have been possible with the support of key professionals, trustees, staff, volunteers, consultants, artists, partner organisations as well as key funders, sponsors and individuals.

In conclusion, we need to take time to reflect on the projects we have implemented, on why we have done what we have done and how we have done it. The outcome of that reflection and the knowledge we take away is the legacy of the women who have run ADAD and one of the gifts the organisation leaves as we go forward. Dance of the African Diaspora is full steam ahead and continues the journey to break barriers in the mainstream in the UK and internationally.

Uchenna Dance presents *The Head Wrap Diaries* at The Place, 2016. Dancer Habibat Ajayi. Photographer Foteini Christofilopoulou.

REFLECTION, REVOLUTION AND RESOLUTION: BLACK DANCE IN THE UK 2000 TO 2016

Wheelchair Duet Co-Mission 2015. Photographer Kathryn Brillhart.

DEBORAH BADDOO

The request to me for a paper was in two parts. Firstly a comment on the visibility and education of Black dance within British cultural practice and, with reference to State of Emergency's Big Mission initiative, to answer the question:

WHAT DO INDEPENDENT AGENCIES BRING TO THE TABLE?

To put this paper into context, I am Artistic Director of State of Emergency Productions, which is a performance and production company, committed to the creation of high quality work and to preservation and innovation in the fields of dance and music and is a National Portfolio Organisation supported by Arts Council England.

State of Emergency (SOE) is an advocate for artists and performers with a national and international perspective. State of Emergency leads by example, as artist/leaders, and forms alliances that support engagement in and appreciation of the arts by a broad cross section of society.

Our mission is to create, present, celebrate, educate, promote, capture, disseminate and archive, and to deliver our vision through the driving force of our creative programme which includes: productions, performances and showcases, choreography and composition, tours and festivals, audio and video recording, leadershtip development, artists' training and professional development and a national archive for Black Dance.

As a producer, State of Emergency has a proven track record and is proud of its associations with some of the leading names in the contemporary arts scene. Across a wide range of activity, State of Emergency has also provided opportunities for hundreds of emerging and established artists and participants in the fields of dance and music.

As a Black female Artistic Director having worked with Black choreographers and dance artists over the last 25 years, I have seen many changes and developments in the sector, as well as experiencing the ongoing dialogue between artists and organisations with regard to the profile, visibility, practice and opportunities for Black dance.

I acknowledge that the use of the term ' Black dance' and 'Black choreographers' is very broad, and that Black dance itself covers a broadness in dance styles and influences.

I also acknowledge the long dialogue the sector has had around terminology, definition and the aesthetic of Black dance and dance of the African Diaspora. It is in these discussions, that one can begin to understand the uniqueness of Black dance in the UK.

In this presentation the term Black dance and Black choreographers refers to artists of African, Caribbean or mixed race heritage, who create and present work in any style format or fusion of styles.

Back in 2001 in response to a huge lack of visibility and education about Black dance forms and in response to personal and collective experience regarding the glass ceiling that seemed to exist in the programming and profile of Black choreographers and their work, State of Emergency set up a programme called The Mission.

The Mission's aims were to

- Showcase new Black choreographic talent
- Develop audiences for dance from the African Diaspora
- Commission the creation of choreography for a debut tour featuring a number of Black dance styles in one event
- Support professional Black dance artists in terms of marketing and support, encouraging funders and venue programmers to attend, in addition to new audiences

Accompanying the Mission tour was a national Roadshow tour that took place in seven UK regions. Its aims were:

- To address the lack of education and training in Black dance forms within the education sector
- To raise the profile of Black dance in education and community forums and to de-mystify Black dance and make it more accessible to the general community in terms of participation and audience
- To provide work opportunities and creative skills development for Black dance artists
- To develop audiences for Black dance
- To support Black dance students in training, who may feel culturally isolated

This strategic intervention seemed to animate the sector and to begin to articulate and pull together a body of thought regarding action necessary for change.

Following the early Mission tours and regional showcases and conferences, State of Emergency undertook research to discover, highlight and support work by professional Black choreographers. State of Emergency uncovered and identified new emerging Black choreographic talent.

The next step followed; The Big Mission project, another State of Emergency initiative which sought to highlight and celebrate the diversity of Black choreographic talent and offered opportunities for artists to create, perform, network, discuss and debate. It was a unique event, the first of its kind in the UK and offered key opportunities for the professional development of Black dance artists, highlighted and focused attention on the state of culturally diverse dance in the UK at that time. It also showcased and celebrated the range and diversity of Black British dance work and exposed a wide range of Black dance to the public and promoters, addressing acknowledged gaps in the programming of culturally diverse dance in the UK. It also provided a unique opportunity for wide networking amongst artists and forums to discuss and debate the needs of the sector.

This was a long awaited high profile opportunity to increase the visibility of the Black dance sector and put down a marker on which to build.

The Big Mission festival event took place in Birmingham in 2005 and Swindon in 2008 and was delivered in partnership with large scale and small scale venues in those cities.

Celebrating the range and diversity of talent, The Big Mission Festival brought artists together with promoters and other industry professionals in a series of networking forums with critical debate on the future of this genre and also offered a key professional development opportunity as there were workshops and masterclasses from internationally renowned Black choreographers/dance artists and a showcase of new and emerging Black dance artists.

This project was planned in direct response to feedback from Black dance artists, who perceived that, in general, culturally diverse dance has been under-represented in dance programming and the needs of the artists were not being met. There appeared to be, and to some extent still is, a perception that an infrastructure for Black Dance does not exist.

In response to the needs of the sector and its desire to increase visibility, this event was part of a planned and strategic approach to providing building blocks to create an infrastructure for Black dance in the UK and to educate the wider public and the mainstream contemporary dance 'power brokers'. This event model set a blueprint for later events of this kind for the Black dance sector.

However, sadly even now the infrastructure is still in its infancy, with small independent organisations such as SOE, ADAD and Irie Dance Theatre struggling within the restraints of funding and the general mainstream dance ecology to continue to fly the flag for Black dance in all its forms and fusions. They play a crucial role in making visible what, still to a large extent, is invisible or ,at best, only partially visible.

Admittedly, over the last two decades there have been many changes and developments in the sector, and I have been part of the ongoing dialogue between artists and organisations with regard to the profile, practice and opportunities for Black dance.

Moving on from this intervention and as a result of this ongoing feedback in 2010, the time felt right for an up to date overview of where Black dance in the UK was at. Initiatives to try and create a level playing field for diversity in dance had come and gone and it was time to take stock. Working against a backdrop of cuts in investment in the arts, it seemed that a probing insight into the state of Black dance in the current climate was well overdue. I was eager to find out whether my perceptions were correct and what, if anything, had fundamentally changed since the last baseline report 'Time for Change' by Hermin McIntosh researching into a framework for African Peoples' dance forms was published in 2000.

As State of Emergency has always strived to be responsive to the Black dance sector and to create opportunities to further development and opportunities, the report 'Altered States' was commissioned and the results of this research directly informed the next five years of part of our programme of work.

Referring back to the question of visibility and education regarding Black dance and drawing on 70 responses from the dance community, the report concluded that there were six key areas that needed to be addressed and that were crucial for a strong infrastructure and a level playing field – Talent Development; Leadership; Recognition; Archiving; Education and Training; and Infrastructure Development.

Under these six headings the recommendations that came out of this report were:

Talent Development

- A need to embed a national 10 year strategy to develop, grow and nurture new and existing talent led by the Black dance sector
- Further training and development opportunities for emerging choreographers in the form of residencies, international exchanges, networks, artistic development and talent hot-housing
- Training and development opportunities for established choreographers to extend their practice, and to 'think bigger', to include choreographic fellowships, space for ideas development and international placements
- A national programme of community dance teacher training to enable those at grassroots, to effectively train and identify talent in community settings

Infrastructure development

- To develop the 'leadership organisations' within the then RFO portfolio, to be underpinned with organisational development opportunities, artistic director training, peer networking opportunities and leadership development support
- Dance agencies to work with the Black dance sector more proactively, to profile, network and platform talent that is new and emerging, as well as the 'talent that is already there'
- Further work to raise the status, profile and visibility of leadership dance organisations and the role models within them
- A strong national network of Black dance practitioners, companies, producers and makers plugged into networks and opportunities
- A national programme to identify, and create pathways for new and emerging grassroots dancers and choreographers currently 'off the radar'

Leadership

- Raise the profile and recognise the work of existing leaders in Black dance
- Nurture existing organisations, and provide proper support to enable the organisations to grow into 'leadership' organisations
- Build a ten year strategy for infrastructure development, resource and knowledge sharing between these 'leadership' organisations

Recognition

- Critical dialogue to recognise the range of styles and aesthetic in Black dance
- Sector-wide critical dialogues to re-shape the term 'contemporary' dance
- A strategic framework supported by the ACE and the national dance agencies to recognise, support and profile Black dancers and choreographers at all stages in their careers

Archive

- Archive and history of Black dance, in its broadest form

Education and training

- To facilitate opportunities for ongoing strategic dialogues with major dance schools

Further partnership development work with dance schools, universities and Centres for Advanced Training (CATS) Schemes.

The recommendations set out in this report were not new and the 'level playing field' was far from being a reality. On undertaking a review of previous literature, it was clear that the Black dance sector has long been calling for the strengthening of its infrastructure in order to nurture its dancers, choreographers, artists, producers, and leaders. Unfortunately, in 2016, the sector is still calling for the same thing.

The early part of the 21st Century saw both the dismantling and then re-building of the Black dance infrastructure. Companies were on the one hand, disinvested and new companies invested in. The sector is therefore still in development. Further work and investment is required to continue to grow the infrastructure for Black dance and independent organisations clearly have a key role to play in this if there is to be any chance of a national infrastructure.

What perhaps is different is that this 21st Century call for infrastructure development is coupled with a call for an intellectual investment in the Black dance infrastructure. The Black dance sector needs to build in confidence, and to enjoy recognition and respect from colleagues within and outside of the Black dance sector.

This calls for conversations around aesthetics, and the notion of what 21st Century contemporary dance is, and whether now is the time to extend its meaning.

Wrapped up in this dialogue are wider questions about how we support new talent into the dance sector, what dance forms we value, how we encourage dancers from a wider talent pool, diversify our dance schools, support our existing talent and archive that which could be lost for generations to come.

In conclusion, this research called for the development of Black dance to be led by the Black dance sector and supported by the wider dance ecology.

Since we commissioned this report State of Emergency has continued to develop part of its programme in direct response to the articulated needs of the Black dance community and to continue to raise the profile and deliver high quality work in the mainstream, together with bespoke opportunities for leadership training, performance , commissioning and showcasing opportunities and talent development initiatives.

However, more investment is needed in multiple development agencies to make a substantial impact on the visibility of the wide range of Black dance forms, artists and companies in the UK.

To continue to move things forward and as an attempt to galvanise the Black dance sector, with an aim of collective support and action for change and widening opportunity, and in response to the Altered States report's recommendations, in January 2011, State of Emergency began formally to discuss the idea of a strategic alliance of Black choreographers and artists and companies.

The Strategic Alliance for Black Dance (SABD) was established to create a forum for dialogue and to support the development of the Black dance sector. It brings to the fore the wider issues concerning the sector and builds programmes of work in response to these issues. It also provides opportunities for networking and the sharing of knowledge, skills and experience and is a vehicle set up in order to enable work that was already being done to be recognised, for artists not to work in isolation, and to facilitate a 'joined-up' approach within the Black dance sector.

At present SABD meets quarterly in London. The aim is to roll out this network to other regions but further investment is needed for this to happen and the full potential of the Strategic Alliance to be realised.

To continue to contribute to the strengthening of the Black dance infrastructure, State of Emergency set up an annual programme of Artistic Directors and Emerging Artistic Directors Retreats to contribute to the development of leadership skills in the sector. These annual three day residencies around the country have been highly successful in providing artistic leaders with an intensive opportunity to reflect and develop, receive personal and career coaching and network in a positive and relaxing environment.

On the opposite end of the scale, to support talent development in the Black dance sector within the confines of a small independent company, State of Emergency started a talent development programme Re-Position in 2013 for dance graduates and early career artists. The aim of the programme is to sustain experienced dancers with technique, choreographic and performance opportunities to support their career development. This programme has been very effective on a short term project basis creating opportunities for artists to perform at festivals and other events and working with a variety of choreographers. However these short low key interventions have relatively small impact and as a long term solution to building a sustainable national model for talent development that specifically targets diverse artists, once again, much more investment is needed as there is a limit to how much small independent organisations can do to address and sustain long term change.

It is unrealistic to expect a few small organisations to be able to address all needs and new independent agencies need to be established to respond to different areas of need.

Love Sex 2014. Photographer Irven Lewis.

THE IMPACT OF AN ARCHIVE

I will now turn to the second part of the brief for this presentation which invited a reflection on the setting up of State of Emergency's Black Dance Archives project, and look at how it may impact and inform future practice.

In 2013 SOE was successful in receiving a major funding bid from the Heritage Lottery Fund to set up the first Black Dance Archive (BDA). This is a landmark project, as there has never been a comprehensive archive for Black dancers and choreographers.

The Black Dance Archive is a bold initiative in response to the lack of a coordinated and coherent archive for Black dance. The project initially aimed to collect up to 10 archives from celebrated individuals and organisations operating in Black dance from the 1960s through to 2001. In fact it has collected 29 archives, such was the response and need.

Accompanying this work, the project has animated the archive through dance with an extensive, informal and formal participation programme, educational resources and a national touring exhibition.

The archive will undoubtedly provide a practical archive resource for the further development of British Black dance in the UK, addressing a huge gap in existing provision for all students and individuals who want to make sense of the history of Black British Dance.

A new academic strand attached to the BDA will also be created using the Archive as a resource that responds to an on-going need to embed Black dance within university research and development and will provide an educational resource to all those interested in Black dance. Once again a single independent organisation can only have capacity to start to create change and begin to address education and visibility in Black dance.

In conclusion, I wish to reflect on the question of visibility. Over the last 20 years there has clearly been a flux in the support and visibility of Black dance.

Most Black artists I know are clear in their desire to be part of the mainstream and take all opportunities that come their way. They want a level playing field for career development opportunities and visibility, but there is still some way to go, even in 2016.

In the cultural landscape there are a number of arts organisations, particularly in London and other major cities, that embrace diversity within their programme and the opportunities that they provide, but there are still a huge number who, for a range of reasons, are still reluctant to lift the barrier of opportunity to engage with diverse work.

As a Black female producer, after so long championing the cause for the visibility and mainstreaming of Black artists and their work, I tested the water with a question at a recent Strategic Alliance Meeting at The Place Theatre and asked the dancers and choreographers present whether they still thought that there was a need to have these Black dance focused meetings.

The response was unanimous in that they felt that a place to meet and share ideas and contacts, a 'safe and supportive space' where artists can be themselves and share the particular issues that are as relevant to them as Black artists now as it might have been 20 years ago.

There is still not sufficient support, visibility and opportunities for Black dancers and choreographic work to be shown and there are not enough independent organisations that support the education and development of the vast range and influences of dance from the diaspora.

In terms of education there is still only one officially accredited training course in African People's Dance in the UK and I am not aware that there is any training at degree level in these forms. Indeed I heard recently that due to the over reliance of universities on income from overseas students even the modules of African Peoples' Dance forms that existed as part of some dance degrees have been discontinued as they are seen as not so relevant for overseas students.

In the absence of any robust infrastructure it is essential that the few independent agencies that do exist to support and develop culturally diverse dance work continue to push the boundaries and address the situation.

However, it is easy to be cynical. After so many years of pushing for opportunities and recognition for Black dancers and choreographers and being part of endless research, debate and numerous initiatives with the Arts Council to understand and address issues of diversity, I feel that at last perhaps a shift has started with the Creative Case for Diversity policies that may force all organisations to be accountable and really reflect and address the issue of diversity in their organisations in clearly demonstrable ways.

Ghettoisation and isolation of the work of Black dancers and choreographers is not the answer. Our wish is to be invited to all the parties on offer and fully participate in the dancing.

THE TALENT IS THERE, THE OPPORTUNITIES ARE NOT

Union Dance Company performing Thomas Pinnock's *Storytime Dance Time* **at the Roundhouse, 20 March 1986. Corrine Bougaard front.** Photographer Dee Conway. © Lebrecht Music & Arts.

HILARY S. CARTY

Thank you to Pawlet for creating this space to meet, cogitate and strategise on how we step out of the barriers. Strategising is important, for it is not enough to just see the barriers and stand still – we need ways to get over or around them.

A couple weeks ago I saw a call from Pawlet on my phone and I was so tempted not to answer because I knew she would be chasing for my, as yet unwritten, draft of this paper. Then it occurred to me that, in chasing me to get the words out of my head and onto paper, Pawlet was doing just what I know needs to be done – going beyond seeing the barriers. Regarding them as 'hurdles' – she was doing her bit to jump them and make us all jump them too. So I answered the phone, and wrote the chapter, and want to begin with thanks to Pawlet. For keeping the flame alive!

When it comes to Black dancers, Black artists or Black art in general, my experience tells me that the talent is there – it's the opportunities that are not.

We lack opportunities to nurture, to grow and to sustain talent; and the imperative for active – or better – pro-active interventions is, for me, crystal clear.

Back in the year 2000 as Director of Dance at Arts Council England, I commissioned a report from Hermin McIntosh, a cultural champion who was one of my first role models for leadership in the arts and someone who is still jumping barriers today. Her report 'Time for Change' highlighted the fragility of the infrastructure for Black dance as a key challenge. It highlighted the need for a multi-faceted approach with artists and activists collaborating to address the issues of development from multiple angles; covering aesthetics, creativity and artform development; presentation and touring; advocacy; strategic development; infrastructural development; and training and education....

That was 16 years ago. I fear that, if I were to commission that report again today we might find a different set of circumstances but, at the core, some very similar conclusions; despite the tremendous talent and ingenuity of our artists, our infrastructure is weaker than it needs to be to support creative talent.

I'll explore the issue of infrastructure more a little later, but I'll start by telling you a little about my own background. Not because I want to brandish my CV, but because I think my own journey, as insecure as it felt at times, actually reveals the importance of some key elements of the leadership, education and empowerment that I've been asked to explore.

Seven key elements stand out for me:

- Exposure
- Ambition
- Training
- Talent
- Opportunity
- Challenge
- Sponsors

I think these are vital aspects of any dance infrastructure that need to be in place if progress is to be made. Some of those elements are in our control, others outside our control, but we should not let them get beyond our reach.

My journey into the arts began with moments of inspiration at school. I was one of the fortunate ones... school visits to many of London's theatres were regularly provided and our annual dance performances soon became a highlight of the school year. Embracing both the professional and community dance fields, I had tremendous exposure to many dance styles and many different aspects of the dance profession – so my sense of what was possible began with a wide field. This exposure opened up dynamic new avenues and new possibilities for a girl from South East London - which is why I am passionate about the intrinsic value of the arts as well as their ability to impact and transform lives.

That initial inspiration soon transformed into ambition – the desire to succeed in this amazing profession. Like many starting out, I wasn't exactly sure what I would do with dance, but I knew I had to find my place; the route to making MY difference by using my particular set of skills and abilities. So that led me to the academic rather than the vocational route. I studied for a degree in Performance Arts, in Leicester (at what is now De Montfort University). Then, following my instincts and the thirst to understand more about my cultural heritage, I studied for a year at the Jamaica School of Dance in Kingston, gaining a Post-Graduate Certificate in Education. I was blessed to work with a number of the 'Greats' of Jamaican dance – Professor Rex Nettleford, Dr. Sheila Barnett, Dr. Barbara Requa, Barry Moncrieffe – they had been at the helm in codifying the Jamaican dance techniques and I learnt, literally, at their feet. Even today, it makes me smile to know that the notes I jotted down late at night to support my understanding of the techniques, formed the basis of my thesis. That thesis became one of those rare things; a text book on Caribbean Dance. 'Folk Dances of Jamaica' was published in 1988 and republished in 2008, a contribution to capturing and sharing our heritage for generations to come.

Those two periods of formal training gave me the underpinning I needed to build my career. I was trained to dance but not simply to move, but also to review, to criticise, to assess and to rationalise. I learned how to judge excellence, and quality. I learnt the benchmarks, the traditions, the norms and exceptions. I could conjure with the forms from both historical and contemporary perspectives.

The bright lights of the auditorium did play a (small) part in my early career, but it was actually behind the scenes where I felt my talent could shine – not even backstage, but off-stage – in administration and management... those hugely unsexy areas! Whilst my colleagues hesitated with application forms and criteria, somehow I was not daunted and quickly learnt to combine my creative dance training with administrative competencies to form a connection or bridge. I could straddle both sides of the practice/policy divide, and have been doing so ever since.

But talent alone is not enough in this or any profession – talent needs exposure and it needs opportunities – to experiment, to learn, to make mistakes and to develop. Being based in the Midlands through the 1980s was one of the best decisions I ever made. The opportunities abounded. Opportunities to create, to perform, to produce and, for me, to facilitate, to nurture and to enable. My role as Dance & Mime Officer for East Midlands Arts (now Arts Council England's East Midland's office) gave me the opportunity to learn and practice my craft – and my craft was 'policy making' – building the context, the infrastructure and the resources for dance to thrive. So it was a pleasure to span the national portfolio and see every version of Black people dancing in evidence: Angie Anderson at Ekome; Judith Palmer at Adzido; Sheron Wray at London Contemporary Dance Theatre and Rambert, Brenda Edwards at English National Ballet... Such range and diversity of Black women dancing...

When, in the 1990s, I took my craft to the national level, as Director of Dance for Arts Council England, I was then able to grapple with some of the sector challenges on the large-scale and for the long-term, to try to put in place some of that infrastructure that every art form needs to thrive.

Working in dance, the performing arts and then the wider arts, provided a decade of leadership, of role modeling, of being challenged and finding my own resilience. I was challenged, both positively and negatively – by the established dance communities who wanted to maintain and enhance the status quo; and challenged by the emerging dance sector who wanted radical shifts in profile, in recognition and in engagement, as well as the crucial funding.

It was tough to find the right balance – but important to continually strive to ensure that the opportunities for the many were not negated by the demands of the few.

I did not manage this on my own. I have had mentors galore. But more importantly, I have also had sponsors. People who have made it their business to ensure I really learnt the ropes of the profession; who were active advocates and champions against the naysayers; and who helped me rationalise the failures and mistakes, without withdrawing their support. Today we are very fond of mentoring, but sometimes we need to intervene more pro-actively to demonstrate our commitment. So if you are in a leadership role, go beyond mentoring and actively sponsor that talent you see before you.

When I consider the issues of leadership, education and empowerment for Black dance artists, I think the picture, in all honesty, is somewhat patchy. Today's Black dance has to be gritty, determined and downright adventurous to achieve that invaluable exposure to a wide field of dance. There are many opportunities to explore a myriad of western or hybrid forms and key dance institutions do support a diverse range of artists to hone their craft... But there are fewer and fewer opportunities to be truly grounded in the techniques at the origin of Black dance.

Union Dance Company performing Thomas Pinnock 's *Storytime Dance Time* at the Roundhouse, 10 February 1987. Corrine Bougaard front. Photographer Dee Conway. © Lebrecht Music & Arts.

So the formational activities of the 80s and 90s such as

- The Black Dance Summer Schools – here in Leicester in the mid 1980s
- The myriad of companies creating work of every dimension:
  - African tradition from Adzido;
  - Caribbean baselines from Irie! Dance Theatre;
  - urban contemporary from RJC;
  - experimentation from Corrine Bougaard's Union Dance Company; or
  - Phoenix Dance Company pushing boundaries with dexterity and style…

That range of expression and opinion is, regrettably, absent from today's UK dance experience. So today's artists have to be yet more ingenious, diligent and committed about how they are underpinning, fuelling and nurturing their craft.

Turning to leadership, we DO have role models and models of good practice within our midst – look at the panels of presenters before you here today – and we could equally be joined by many in the audience. Our challenge is not the absence of leadership, but the absence of recognition. We buy in too readily to the disposable culture of the Primark Generation (other retailers are also available!) and we neither look back at those who have gone before, nor elevate those who are here now – so we throw away our leaders in search of 'the new', the latest or the next, innovation. In my view, those are false choices. We can and should acknowledge both.

So I warmly appreciate ADAD's 'Life-time Achievement Awards' and LDIF's annual corralling of the sector around the issues that concern us in these critical opportunities for reflection and discourse. We need these moments to consider, acknowledge and reflect; to build and celebrate our markers of leadership both past and present.

In the field of education this moment feels like one of pause. The statistics for BAME individuals in academia as a whole are pretty woeful, so the arts are by no means isolated in having few examples of Black academic investigation. All the more reason, methinks, to pay tribute to those who have made inroads.

So let's acknowledge Beverly Glean – Artistic Director of Irie! Dance Theatre – who pioneered the UK's first Diploma in African and Caribbean Dance, accredited by the University of Birkbeck and delivered in partnership with City & Islington College. Beverley was also at the helm of creating the Dance Foundation Degree in 2008 – working in partnership with City and Islington College and London Metropolitan University to create a syllabus that placed Dance of the African Diaspora right alongside contemporary and classical dance in the formal education context. And the alumni from both those programmes are absolutely contributing to the vocabulary and creative voice of today's dance artists.

Another creative artist who has grappled with the challenge of academia is the 'H' Patten, who lectured at the University of Surrey. Now 'H' is, of course, not a woman in dance – but I know from the course alumni how much his contribution was valued as a unique joining of tradition and creativity in African and Caribbean dance and his PhD Dancehall, a genealogy of spiritual practices in Jamaican dance – is set to make another dynamic contribution to our understanding of our contribution to the arts and society.

'Funmi Adewole, also studying for a PhD in British Dance and the African Diaspora at De Montfort University; and Adesola Akinleye at Middlesex University also deserve our acknowledgement, for building that critical discourse around the arts of the African diaspora. For as Beverly Glean observed in creating the Foundation degree; we need the literature, the critique and the academic underpinning so that our arts can also contribute to the education of future generations.

Highlighting these achievements in the formal education sector is, I know, only part of the story. The stalwart activities in the informal sector grows the grassroots and set the seeds for many of us. Both are important. Both build profile and create legacy. But in this society what gets measured gets noticed and a crucial unit of measurement is that of academic discourse. Let's stay in that conversation and let our voices be heard.

So that leads me to the issue of empowerment.

One of the things I did to get information for my paper was to email a few contacts and ask:

- What's your experience?
- Who has influenced your career?
- What is or should be in place?

The responses could collectively be summed up as 'disheartening'. We desperately need to consolidate our efforts - or many of the key gains, that have been made, will continue to be eroded.

- Who is to empower whom? I find myself asking? Who decides? What are their credentials? What gives them authority? Or legitimacy? What are they doing 'in my name'?

We need to look critically at our leadership and at our education, otherwise we may find that we are giving away our power, rather too cheaply.

Can we empower ourselves? Can we decide, determine and deliver? Can we build and consolidate the networks that create an 'infrastructure'? How active is our individual and collective engagement with what we have, even whilst we focus on what we want?

So I'm grateful to Pawlet Brookes for persisting, for making HER difference, with the conferences, the publications, the incubation of artists and the exposure to performance created by the Let's Dance International Frontiers. I'm grateful to ADAD for the Trailblazers; Bloom and the Open Stage Platforms. I'm grateful to State of Emergency for supporting artists networks and capturing our archives in the British Black Dance Archives project, funded by the Heritage Lottery Fund. I'm grateful to the artists who, despite the challenges, are still bursting through to share their talents.

Without a stronger infrastructure, they are 'doing it for themselves' and paying a heavy price. So we need more. Plain and simple. If we look back at those core requirements, yes, we have the ambition; and talent. And yes we do indeed have the challenge. But we need more of the elements with our direct control; more exposure, more training, more opportunity and more active sponsors. We have made gains in the past, and can do so for the future, but it needs proactive engagement.

We each need to be playing our part.

BLACK WOMEN IN DANCE STEPPING OUT OF THE BARRIERS

THE DANCE OF LEADERSHIP

Alvin Ailey professional dancers and youth dancers perform for *Black History Month* at the White House. Photographer Cheriss May/NurPhoto/Getty Images.

MAUREEN SALMON

"The things we truly love stay with us always, locked in our hearts as long as life remains." These words of Josephine Baker resonate with my passion for the leadership of dance.

This paper is personal perspective, based on a thirty year journey, captured through different roles in dance, cultural and creative industries and wider society. During those three decades, I have reinvented, rebranded and repositioned myself several times to create new futures and legacies that I am proud to share. This journey would not have been possible without friendships, relationships and the leadership of others. The paper gives prominence to Black women in dance whose leadership has been inspirational and aspirational.

Dance has always been important in the lives and history of Black women, and the Black community. Michelle Obama echoed this when she hosted a Black History Month event at the White House in February 2016 to highlight the contributions African American women have made to dance in the USA. Imagine such an event at Number 10 Downing Street or the Palace of Westminster.

Within the UK, there has been a proliferation of Black women who have contributed to the development of the dance ecosystem/ecology that exist today, but they have not been recognised or become part of the history and culture of dance. Doris Harper-Wills, storyteller, writer and choreographer is one of those women. Doris was my first dance teacher, role model and mentor. I admired her passion, courage, tenacity and personal style and brand. It was in 1976 while studying for my A levels that I started taking Caribbean dance classes at the Commonwealth Institute, London where Doris worked as member of the education team. Since arriving in the UK from Jamaica in 1972, this was the first time I felt reconnected with my Caribbean identity and heritage. It was also a new beginning to being part of the British arts and cultural community. Doris reminisced the experience on 20 March 2008.

FOR MAUREEN'S FIFTIETH

Do you remember ole times, dear Maureen?

Do you remember ole times?

The twisting and the twirling

Of the fingers that entranced

The swinging and the swirling

Of the skirts when we danced;

The wining and the whirling,

The bouncing and the flouncing,

By you Aylestone (high school) girls from Brent

Oh yes, you were heaven sent

To the C.I.

In Kensington High.

Do you remember the names, dear Maureen?

Do you remember the names?

Remembering those names made me feel catatonic,

To remember those names I devised a mnemonic.

Vivienne Townsend, Ethol Ugeji,

Jennifer Dale, Openibo Patti,

Eunice Dennis, Dotlyn Johnson,

Barbara Taylor, Anas Allison,

Ruth Jarman, Roxanne Carrington,

Joan Fred, Grace Walker,

Maureen Salmon.

We did Queen's Jubilee in 1977

Chiswick House Grounds – performance was a gem!

We drove through London in my Black limousine

Liveried chauffeur – courtesy of the Queen.

We also did the river cruise with me at the helm!

Oh, how we danced! – performance was a gem

We danced at The Royal Commonwealth Society too

Wait a minute, Maureen, that's where we are right now!

We've come full circle Maureen, do join me, take a bow!

One's never too old to celebrate.

Let's do it now before it's too late.

The twisting and the twirling

Of the fingers that entranced;

The swinging and the swirling

Of the skirts when we danced;

The wining and the whirling,

The bouncing and the flouncing,

Let's do it now until we drop

Not because we're older we should stop!

All rights reserved © Doris Harper-Wills 2009

In 2013, Doris became the architect of her legacy. Her book 'The Wings of Iere' was published to mark her eightieth birthday. At eighty five years old, Doris performed at the Guyana 50th Independence Anniversary celebrations in London and was given an award for her contributions to the Guyanese community. Doris has been my leading light.

The 1970s and the 1980s were critical times in the politics and history of the Black arts and cultural leadership. Within months of starting the Caribbean dance classes, I had the opportunity to attend a lecture demonstration by Arthur Mitchell, the founder artistic director of the Dance Theatre of Harlem at the New London Theatre, and also saw a performance of the South African musical, Ipi Tombi at Her Majesty's Theatre, London West End. These two diverse dance experiences had a significant impact on my life and future career. I discovered what Ken Robinson, the educationalist, in his book 'The Element: How Finding Your Passion Changes Everything' describes the 'element' as being where passions and natural aptitudes meet.

I took Arthur Mitchell's advice and started to learn about dance through dancing, attending performances and researching. At a conference on Caribbean literature, I recall Earl Lovelace talking about dance as an affirmative gesture which helps people to reclaim their sense of being. Dance is a natural human activity which defines who we are. For me, dance was a means to spiritual, emotional, social, educational and economic well-being. It's what Martha Graham described as the "hidden language of the soul".

BLACK WOMEN IN DANCE STEPPING OUT OF THE BARRIERS

Doris Harper-Wills and Maureen Salmon.

Dance has enabled me to develop the personality traits of a leader, these have influenced my leadership practices and enabled me to be an advocate for social, cultural, economic change and inclusion in society. There is correlation between dance and leadership and it has been researched and documented by Robert B. Denhardt and Janet V. Denhardt (2006) in The Dance of the Leadership, where they make the case for leadership being an art and not a science. They bring together the experiences of artists, musicians, especially dancers, on the one hand, leaders in business, government and society, on the other, to clarify the artistic elements of leadership. At the 'Black Women in Dance' conference, it was interesting to hear Jawole Willa Jo Zollar articulate her perspective on the concepts and practices of the dance of leadership. The contributions of Black women in dance are synonymous with their leadership. Our ability to lead is a personal thing and leading is a natural human activity that is part of all of us (Steve Radcliff, 2012). As Black women, our leadership in dance has significant impact in wider political, economic, social and cultural contexts.

STUDENT LEADERSHIP

As student of dance and education at Roehampton Institute of Higher Education (now Roehampton University) in the 1980s , I became interested in the concept of 'Black dance' as an area of academic research. My motivation was the lack of a culturally diverse dance curriculum reflecting the contemporary British dance scene and my personal experience. On 22 May 1986 to be precise, I presented my thesis on the development of 'Black dance' (Caribbean and African dance, the main dance forms being practiced by people of the African diaspora) in Britain during the period, 1946 to 1986. The time span was determined by significant historical, social, political and artistic events. First, during the 1940s, the dances of Africa and the Caribbean became of interest to Katherine Dunham and Pearl Primus, academics, dancers and anthropologists, who studied and incorporated these dances into theatre dance. Both toured their work to Britain with great success. Second, in 1946 Berto Prushak, the Jamaican dancer, influenced by Dunham and Primus, founded Ballet Nègres, Britain's first all-Black dance company.

The findings gathered from a postal questionnaire which was sent to some 40 dance companies across Britain who had identified with the concept of 'Black dance' was empowering. There was a buoyant dance culture and community championed by Black women who were leading dance companies as well contributing to the development of the dance infrastructure. The pioneers of this period included: Corrine Bougaard, Hilary Carty, Beverly Glean, Jeanefer Jean-Charles, Greta Mendez, Hermin McIntosh, Maggie Semple, Carole Straker to name a few. Over the years, I have observed how these visionary women have become great artistic, educational and organisational leaders and mentors, not just in dance and cultural and creative industries, but within the wider UK society.

DANCE LEADERSHIP

The thesis was a launch pad for my career. Shortly after graduating from Roehampton, I got a job at Adzido while I studied for my Masters in Arts Management at City University. It was an exciting time in the development of Adzido with is its 35-strong ensemble of musicians and dancers. There was a talented group of female dancers, including Judith Palmer.

A consultant was commissioned to produce a strategic development plan to transform Adzido from a community project to a professional company. I spoke of the business case and moral imperative for Black leadership in the organisational development to achieve long term artistic and economic sustainability. In hindsight, I realised I was ahead of my time. I left Adzido to complete my MA thesis 'More Questions Than Answers: A Review of Black Arts Funding and Marketing in Britain'.

Following a brief, but eventful period, as an arts officer for the London Borough of Camden, I was appointed for the dance officer job at South East Arts Board (now Arts Council South East) (1990-1997). During my seven year tenure, I led on the development of the infrastructure for dance and facilitated the successful positioning of the dance community to take on the leadership challenge for dance with the region.

I was also responsible for cultural diversity and delivered an artist-led programme including a three day festival in West Sussex, entitled FRESH, a new perspective on contemporary British arts and culture. FRESH was controversial and stimulated political debate in the media about its relevance to region. I presented the cultural diversity project as a model of good practice at the Race Towards the Millennium conference at the Royal Society of Arts. Delia Barker, an Arts Council dance trainee administrator with Arts Admin, was the assistant producer of FRESH . Delia is currently the director of English National Ballet School and a former dance officer for London Arts Board.

I continued to contribute to the development of dance of the African diaspora and was a board member and chair of Badejo Arts (1990-2000). It was a privilege to work with Peter Badejo, the artistic director. During our ten year partnership, Badejo Arts produced seven international summer schools, six productions and launched a platform for emerging African dance chorographers. The most celebrated was 'The Heart of Dance' a kind of juxtaposition of Joseph Conrad's book 'Heart of Darkness' and the story of Black peoples' journey to the UK. The site specific performance was a boat journey along the river Thames from Greenwich to the London Southbank Centre, where a new Britain was created on the terrace.

Despite a track record of achievements for dance and cultural diversity in the region that had a national impact, it was apparent that there was a lack of access to professional development and career progression opportunities into senior leadership for Black professionals, not just in dance, but also in the wider cultural and creative sector industries. This made me sharpen my focus, with sound advice from within and outside of dance and the arts and cultural sector. I took a quantum leap and migrated to where my talents and strengths were going to be of greater value, where I could develop and grow as a leader and help create new futures.

CULTURAL LEADERSHIP

My transition began with a secondment to the Arts Council of England's Lottery Department Stabilisation Unit. This was preparation for my next job role as director of the cultural strategies for Talent & Skills 2000 (TS2K ,1997-2001), a major pan-London employability project for unemployed young people, many of whom were from Black and ethnic minority backgrounds to work in the new emerging and rapidly growing creative industries. TS2K afforded me the autonomy and was a platform for realising a critical element in my personal manifesto to influence learning and career development of future generations within the creative industries. One of the projects that I was involved in was 'Mind the Gap', a conference held at the Institute of Contemporary Art, co-designed by TS2K young people and professionals from the creative industries . In his welcome message, the chairman of TS2K, Lord Victor Adebowale CBE said Mind the Gap was the start of the transformation of the fastest growing industries in the 21st century. The conference was about designing the future and ensuring that young people were involved in the designing of their futures.

Today, the creative industries are still the fast growing industries in the UK and globally. New figures published by the Department of Culture Media and Sport in January 2016, revealed that the UK's creative industries are now worth £84.1 billion per year to the UK economy. However, various research shows that there is still an under-representation of Black and ethnic minority professionals including Black women in the creative industries, particularly in leadership roles.

The impact of my contribution to the work of TS2K gave me credibility and visibility in the creative industries and wider UK society in a way that dance did not. My work was acknowledged through 'Women of the Year' in 2000 at the 'Millennium Festival of Women's Work', the European Federation of Black Women Business Owners 'Professional Award', and as finalist in the Arts and Media category of the 'European Union Women of Achievement Awards 2001' for my "contributions to pan-European understanding and progress, as well as providing inspiration to others". I thank Naseem Khan, author of 'The Art Britain Ignores' (1976), for nominating me for this award.

These accolades influenced the Foundation for Community Dance to invite me to write about my life in dance. In spring 2000 my article 'Journeys and Discoveries' chronicling my experience in dance and the cultural sector, was published. At the time of writing the article, I was in the process of my reinvention, rebranding and repositioning for a career as an independent consultant. My message to the dance community was:

"For the dance sector to truly flourish in the 21st century it needs to recruit, develop and retain the best talent in the terms of artists and managers from Britain culturally diverse communities and adapt a strategy of leadership and leadership development. The sector would need to be creative and innovative in this endeavour".

POLITICAL LEADERSHIP

TS2K awarded me a fellowship to support my transformation from employee to social entrepreneur/consultant to continue my work in the wider political arena to help achieve economic prosperity for those most excluded from professional education and employment. It was this capacity that the USA based National Black MBA Association commissioned me to research and create its European operation; Black MBA Association (UK) to support the creation of economic wealth and academic excellence and to achieve greater economic diversity in Europe. I forged partnerships with the UK and EU governments, business schools, corporations, business development agencies and social enterprises. The result was an investment in knowledge and skills transfer and substantial funds to co-design and deliver a professional education programme in leadership and entrepreneurship for Black and ethnic minorities from across different industry sectors.

On reflection, this was the kind of strategic thinking, intervention, investment and partnership that dance and the cultural sector was lacking. But it was not long before the Cultural Leadership Programme (CLP) was launched in 2006 under the leadership of Hilary Carty. As a consultant and programme partner to CLP, I contributed to the development of Peach Work-based Placements and was the architect of the Powerbrokers International Leadership Placements (PILP). Delia Barker was awarded a placement at the Errol Barrow Centre for Creative Imagination, University of the West Indies where she was involved in researching a framework for mapping the economic value of the cultural industries in Barbados.

EDUCATIONAL LEADERSHIP

The most effective way to influence the future is through the education of the next generations. Having majored in education as an undergraduate, and guest lecturing from the year dot, in 2005 I researched and studied the teaching and learning in higher and professional education. Since then I have been developing a portfolio of work in higher education in the UK and internationally that complements my consulting work.

As a result of taking the CLP programme to African and the Caribbean, I was invited as a visiting lecturer at the Errol Barrow Centre for the Creative Imagination, University of the West Indies and the International School of Management, Senegal. I teach leadership, management and entrepreneurship at both institutions. At the EBCCI, I teach their dance graduates on the MA in Creative Arts Management programme.

I am now in my second academic year lecturing at the University of the Arts at the London College of Communication, School of Design and the London College of Fashion. As course leader for the BA Design Management and Cultures, and associate lecture on EMB (Fashion) and the MA in Fashion Design Management, I lecture on professional practice in leadership, entrepreneurship, design management and creative industries.

I was invited by the Deputy Vice Chancellor, UAL Race Champion to become part of the Race Champion Forum, where I continue to advocate for culture change and leadership to address the under-representation of the Black and ethnic minorities academics and senior leaders across the University. Recently, I participated in the Race Diversity Week which was primarily led by Black women, both students and staff.

As I write this paper I am in the process of reinventing, rebranding and repositioning myself in the world of academia and continuing my consultancy practice. I am aligning my values, vision and objectives to UAL's. This is anopportunity for me to continue to research, write and document my legacy.

Writing this paper has really made me reflect and value the power of dance. Finally to Judith Palmer, Mercy Nabirye, former chair and director respectively of the Association of Dance of the African Diaspora. Judith and the legacy of Adzido and Mercy have demonstrated professionalism and courageous leadership in steering ADAD through the merger with One Dance UK. When they approach me for advice, I gave my perspective on the merger and provided coaching support to Mercy. In December 2015 Mercy wrote:

"Dear Maureen, this is to let you know my pleasure to have known you. I am thankful for enabling me; as I continue my professional career journey. You have given me the courage to stand tall and strong at several moments along the way and I believe, I am on a new level".

Black Women in Dance: Stepping out of the Barriers was a stage to perform our stories, create new histories and futures. My gratitude to Pawlet Brookes and her team. We first met in 1990 and our paths have crossed many times since.

The world is constantly changing, the creative industries are expanding, the global market place is over-crowded with talents and, so, we must be prepared to continuously review and refresh our brand and market position. As Black women, not just in dance, but in the wider social context, the issue of identify is as important in 2016 21st Century as it was in the 1970s. Jessica Walker's performance of Tick the Box, performed in the context of the conference on 10th May and Yami Rowdy Lofvenberg's performance of Other in One Dance UK's New Shoots Trailblazers Starters Showcase performed on 12th May, at the Place Theatre, London, illustrates and illuminate the debate and the different perspectives.

The future is ours, so how do we as Black women:

- Create a legacy of dance in the Black community and the wider cultural and creative industries sectors that are artistically, culturally, socially empowering and economically sustainable?

- Support the leadership development of the next generations of Black women in dance?

- Construct a strategic and influential sustained Black voice in the UK dance scene and the wider social, cultural and creative industries?

SEVEN LEARNING POINTS FOR SELF-CONFIDENCE

1. Know and stick to your values
2. Discover and intentionally use your strengths
3. Develop a strategic, entrepreneurial mind-set and emotional balance
4. Create an action plan with a three to five year horizon
5. Learn from others' experiences, get a mentor and/or coach
6. Understand the external context: political, economic, social, technological, legal, environmental, nationally and internationally
7. Focus, say no to opportunities that don't play to your strengths or fit with your plans. Don't tick the box, if it does not add value!

INFRASTRUCTURE

Pamela Johnson in *Solo*, choreographed by Neville Campbell, 1990. Photographer Terry Cryer/Phoenix Dance Theatre.

PAM JOHNSON

I have been with Arts Council England for 12 1/2 years working in a handful of roles and places; as Dance Officer in the North West, as Relationship Manager, Dance in Yorkshire and now as a Senior Relationship Manager in London. I've taken part in countless conversations with colleagues and with arts and culture sectors about infrastructure; usually talking about funding, funding programmes, funding applications, buildings and organisations. I've participated in discussions about place, diversity, partnerships with other sectors, training… I've monitored and fed back to organisations on artistic performance, governance, management, financial resilience, leadership, talent development, innovation and risk….I could go on but, in short…I've had countless conversations, with many people, about this abstract thing we term 'infrastructure'.

Being asked to speak today led me to reflect on what infrastructure means and has meant to me. Before, during and surrounding my career; what and where was the infrastructure for me when I started on this journey towards and into dance? What were those key infrastructural elements that helped me navigate challenges and opened doors; that supported the development of my career and my ongoing development as a person?

I allowed myself to reflect on these questions, perhaps in a way that I've never really done before, and I engaged close family and friends in some of the process.

HERE IS A SELECTION AND SUMMARY OF MY REFLECTIONS.

When I was a dancer with Phoenix Dance Theatre, my short programme biography might say that I was introduced to dance at Harehills Middle School aged 10 years old. That was the easy story to tell; and intended for an audience that I perceived either didn't want to hear about or wouldn't understand the part of me that emanated from a working class and quite close-knit diverse, inner city community in Leeds. However, my introduction to dance goes further back than that.

My Mum loved music, mostly Reggae but occasionally Country & Western that she'd play on the 'gram' in the front room. I remember that I'd sometimes go with her to buy her 7in records or LPs from 'Sir Yank's', a record shop set up in a converted garage down the road from us. He always had the latest imports from Jamaica.

Mum enjoyed people and she loved to dance, she'd throw a party once a month on a Saturday night. When we were supposed to be tucked up in bed at the top of the house, I would sneak down to be among the 'big people', enjoy the music and dance. I must have been around five years old. That was probably my first inkling that I enjoyed performing. Family has been and remains a critical component of my infrastructure.

Jamaica Society Leeds was founded by a community of elders in the late 1970s; Jamaican immigrants many of who came to the UK in the 50s and 60s. It's purpose, to celebrate Jamaican culture in the UK. The Society grew from a strong foundation of community organisation, faith and leadership that would deliver regular events in and around Chapeltown, Leeds including dinner dances and annual family coach trips to different parts of the UK. Community elder Mrs Armstrong, called 'Grandma' by the community kids and 'Mother' by our parents, would bring the kids together to teach us traditional folk songs of Jamaica. We would create dances to go with the songs and we'd perform at community events. This community 'organisation' played host to Cindy Breakspeare, after she was crowned the first Black Miss World in 1976. We sang our songs and danced for her and later for the Queen (with our red, white and blue headscarves) when she visited Leeds as part of her 1977 Silver Jubilee tour. Community was and is another important element of my infrastructure.

In 1977 I became a pupil at Harehills Middle School where I met a formidable woman, Nadine Senior; she was my PE teacher and would, years later, go on to become a close friend. At Harehills, dance was on the curriculum for every child, creative dance, not technique. Dance classes took place in a dilapidated gym at the centre of the school surrounded by classrooms. The light was poor, the floor was hard but at the time we didn't know better and better facilities just weren't available; certainly not where we lived. In your fourth and final year at the school, you could choose to join the dance group and create a production that was performed for parents and the local community.

The school introduced us to professional dance and professional dancers. Former pupils such as Darshan Singh Bhuller and Neville Campbell would return to the school to teach a class. We met Namron for the first time; like Darshan, a dancer with London Contemporary Dance Theatre (LCDT) and he was from Jamaica! Bob Cohan and other members of the company also paid us a visit whenever they were touring to Leeds. We would have the opportunity to see LCDT and Ballet Rambert performances at the Leeds Grand Theatre. Infrastructure contribution? Opportunities to create and perform, access to professional artists, professional performance and above all, their unyielding generosity.

Once you left the school and went onto high school, there were very few opportunities to continue dancing so that formidable PE teacher at Harehills, Nadine Senior, established the Harehills Youth Dance Company where past pupils could return to the school on Tuesday and Thursday evenings to create work to dance, occasionally to work with professional artists and perform the work at venues across the UK. Imagine, kids from our community performing at Sadler's Wells and the Royal Opera House alongside the likes of Royal Ballet, London Festival Ballet, Ballet Rambert and LCDT. Here was an opportunity to step beyond what you know and celebrate what you can do and we're still only 13, 14, 15 years old.

Older members of the group and former Harehills Youth Dance Company members progressed into dance training but the only places you could train as a dancer were in or close to London, 200 miles away. So the very same PE teacher established the Northern School of Contemporary Dance (NSCD) which launched in 1985 with its first cohort of 13 students. I was one of them. Infrastructure? Local opportunity for progression to vocational dance training created in large part by a teacher's vision and her support.

BLACK WOMEN IN DANCE STEPPING OUT OF THE BARRIERS 57

Pam Johnson for Northern School of Contemporary Dance. Photographer Terry Cryer.

Pamela Johnson in *Sacred Space* choreographed by Phillip Taylor, 1991. Photographer Kieron Vital/Phoenix Dance Theatre.

In 1988 I was leaving for London for a year of additional training at the London Contemporary Dance School and, one week before I left, I was asked if I would return in a year's time to become one of the first females to join Phoenix alongside fellow Harehills pupils and friends Seline Thomas, Dawn Donaldson and Sharon Donaldson. And we did.

I 'retired' from performing in 1998 and after a short time as a freelancer and a year with Kokuma Dance Theatre in Birmingham, Nadine Senior suggested that I apply for a role at the NSCD as their Outreach Development Manager. Infrastructure? Signposting to and local employment. Seeing my potential. Trust.

Leap forward a few years and 2003 delivered probably THE most significant event in my life. My Mum passed away. And this was at the same time that my role at the NSCD was made redundant. It was incredible to have the support of friends, many of who attended Mum's funeral. It was after the funeral, when most of my family had returned home to their respective corners of the world, that I suddenly found myself rudderless. My confidence was fractured and I felt alone in determining what to do next. After busying myself organising Mum's funeral and with no job should I now take good time out to grieve or apply for jobs in roles that no one was signposting me to; that no one was encouraging me to go for? I like to believe that I drew from one of our parent's greatest gifts to us, resilience, and the lesson we all instinctively picked up early on: 'you want something, you must work for it'. I took myself to the library and searched for jobs. I wasn't ready or prepared to leave the world of dance and so I was drawn to an advert from Arts Council England in Manchester which was looking for a Dance Officer. I applied, to be strictly honest, for the practice. By the time I returned home I took a call offering me the job. It was September and I started the role in November. Self-resilience.

I'd been with the Arts Council for a few weeks and I recall that after a short time I took a call and shortly afterwards received a visit from another Arts Council colleague, Delia Barker, now the Chief Executive of English National Ballet School. Delia wanted to make sure that I was okay and settling in. She made a connection which I understood immediately, I wasn't the only Black woman working in dance at the Arts Council and I had her support.

My reflections confirmed that key infrastructural elements for me were, and still are (among other things):

- Family and Community – people to learn from and grow with;
- A supportive yet formidable teacher, and later a friend, who gave opportunity to create, perform and progress;
- Generosity of professionals who opened their experience and practice to us and inspired;
- Signposting to employment, seeing your potential before you do, investment and trust;
- Self-resilience;
- Support

My reflections also drew out an important theme. Whilst I accept that funding, buildings, etc. can be important, the most important part of any infrastructure is its people: How we treat ourselves, as a whole with all your life experiences that come with that; how we relate to others and learn, adapt and grow; and how we treat each other with generosity, respect, our capacity to advocate and for openness.

How we relate to each other really matters; giving life, meaning and value to all the other inanimate things that we all talk about when we talk about 'infrastructure'.

SEVEN STAGES OF CREATING

Catherine Dénécy in *Unpeubeaucoupalafoliepasdutout*, in Paris 2013. Photographer Philippe Virapin.

CATHERINE DÉNÉCY

INTRODUCTION

I was invited to join this conversation by being asked to talk about the creativity I have discovered, explored and found as a Black woman dancing, as a creole woman in the dance world. Here I share with you how I have stepped out of the *barriers* that had unfortunately been set out for me. I am glad to have the opportunity to talk about my journey and deconstruct what made me into creative thinker, dancer and art maker that I am today. But I realise that to genuinely do so, I need to identify the barriers that have been on my path, what *mechanisms* put them in place and which *process* allowed me to jump over them and set my creative self free.

As I started to think about a way to talk about those barriers, my relationship to them and how I found myself stepping over them, I had to genuinely analyse my journey in dance, from my very first dance class at the age of 5 to the last performance I gave of my own work, at the launch of Let's Dance International Frontiers 2016 at age 30. As I thought of all the dance classes I took, the companies I have danced with and the work I have created, the different stages of my career started reminding me of a model I had heard about a few years ago: the Kubler-Ross Model. This model is probably more familiar to you as the seven stages of grief. Then I thought "Hold on, why are you going to compare your art to grieving? Your art is joyful, your art is making! Why have the idea of death?" I thought it was crazy to compare finding my creative self with the process of grieving! But I looked further and found out that this model of grieving is not only used to understand the mechanisms that occur in the case of death of a loved one, but also to help positively heal from a lost amorous relationship or from substance abuse or whilst going through divorce.

Dance has been and will always be my lover, it is the thing for which I will give up anything, move to the other side of the world for in a minute. Dance is like a drug sometimes, it keeps you up at night. It is a beautiful drug I want to abuse. Moreover coming to own my dance has asked me to reprogramme myself many times and divorce with beliefs that I had been married to since a very young age. Thus I found a reason to go further in the comparison of my process with the 7 stages. Love, abuse, divorce... I had the key words, I could go for it and analyse my path using this model, but before I dived into it I wondered if my stakes were high enough to be compared to the previous examples, or was I just being dramatic about all of this? But it occurred to me that everything about my accomplishment in dance had its true share of drama, and I literally had to fight (sometimes people, often ideologies) to be able to make a career in dance!

I have always known that my dance, this said lover and drug, would end up being taken away from me if I didn't find my place, my legitimacy and a way to have access to it. The title of this publication says it all, I think it's fair to say that any successful Black woman in dance MUST be a survivor of some kind. I want to have a clear vision and an understanding now of the wars, the battles and the fields I have survived or will have to successfully win over in my future.

So I propose to talk to you about my dance journey while using the model of the seven stages of grief and share with you how I (wrongly) learnt to dance DESPITE OF my true identity and body to finally end up dancing OUT of it; then how I was taught to dance IN it, had to accept dancing WITH it and finally came to dance FOR and THROUGH it.

STAGE 1: SHOCK – *INITIAL PARALYSIS AT HEARING THE BAD NEWS*

I didn't choose dance, it was prescribed to me. Literally. at the age of five, I was diagnosed with lordosis, commonly called swayback posture which caused me to frequently have tremendous pain in my neck. The medication offered to me at that time was 30 hours of physical therapy where I was introduced to the art of "tucking" with great success, and the doctor also said I should take ballet classes. Overnight, my Wednesdays took on a whole new meaning; in the morning this very nice white woman was desperately teaching me how standing straight was not what I thought it was and that I had to curve my pelvis inward (all the time!) in order to fix my devious spine. In the afternoons, I was at a ballet barre learning all the arms shapes, torso and head movements to support and honour my newly found habit of tucking. It was a complete day.

I always say I didn't choose ballet, ballet chose me. It was the medication, the fixer, the only dance form that could "straighten" me so I could finally be "right". Now when I research about lordosis and its cures I see the words; planks, lunges, crunches, core support, lengthen, strengthen. I see actions. But the message I learnt 25 years ago was that something was wrong with me; I learnt that my spine wasn't naturally right. I had to work hard on who I was to deserve my spot at the barre as I came to ballet class as the "sick one" and I learnt that of all dances ballet was the master and the saviour (it had to be, the doctor strongly advised it, and he can save lives!!).

Why is this comparable to the stage of shock and initial paralysis? Because from that time, from this starting point of ballet dance, I lost the freedom of my spine. My spine was born free and needed lengthening and strengthening but there I was taught that it needed straightening and locking. My spine didn't gain in freedom then, whereas the movement of my spine became relevant in my capacity of not moving it too much, of not letting it do whatever it pleased, of forcing it into positions that were actually limiting it. Moreover I was taught that this was the right way of dancing, and most of all, of being.

This is my shock, my loss, this is what I had to grieve, the loss of freedom of my spine; the brain of my dancing body, and the introduction of the belief in my actual brain that it was the only way to dance and the condition for standing on stage in front of people.

After a year of physical therapy and ballet classes, my swayed back was healed. I was a hard-working girl and I wanted the fix because I feared the pain, so I danced strong, held the ballet barre hard, and tucked my pelvis good all day every day. But why stop? I had shown some great abilities in ballet class, I had a new way other than my school work to be a good girl, my path was set, and I would keep dancing. But I must not forget that I wasn't born the right way to do it, so I should carefully listen to my ballet teacher, that by substitution it would become over the years the doctor.

Catherine Dénécy in *Unpeubeaucoupalafoliepasdutout*, in Paris 2013. Photographer Philippe Virapin.

STAGE 2: DENIAL – *TRYING TO AVOID THE INEVITABLE*

Fast forward, I am now 14. It is clear that by now there is no doubt in my mind that no dance other than ballet deserved my attention and effort. After all the time and hard work of trying to fit in the spinal mould of ballet aesthetics, it was as if I had made a personal investment, and I had to watch over it. I had no other will than go forward with it, go further in it, and keep doing it DESPITE OF my naturally devious body.

It's in this mental landscape that came the time where I discovered that I really loved dancing, it was more than a hobby, it was a calling, and maybe something I could be "allowed" to do for a living! It all went very fast. I won my first ballet dance competition in Guadeloupe, (First prize! I was a hard worker, as I said). As a result of my performance at this competition I also won a scholarship to study at the Alvin Ailey School in New York City for two months that summer.

Ailey?! Me?! It was a real shock, I had never known of Black people dancing. So far, I had just been trying to copy the white long, lean, beautiful body of my ballet teacher. I went to New York with my mom, and everything changed, Black beautiful women in ballet class, I was no longer the only Black person in class, AND there was more to dance than just ballet! I discovered Graham, Horton and Jazz. In Jazz, the music sounded like the music I heard on the radio, in Horton, the drums reminded me of the drums from Guadeloupe and in Graham, my spine, this beautiful straight and locked, "please don't sway again!" thing, could move in a very narrow manner.

 I came back home with a new goal, to become an Alvin Ailey dancer. At Ailey some type of freedom had been brought to me in my dance aesthetics and I had seen dancers that looked like me. I had no reason to not believe that I could be one of them if I worked hard enough. I had found my purpose.

What I didn't understand at the time is that I had not been freed from anything. I spoke earlier about dance being a drug. I had just found a new dealer. The content of my dancing was different but the containers, the barriers, were all the same. In fact, it became even worse. Now I had a career plan, the mind starts calculating by the time I was 18 years old, a high-school graduate, on my way to New York to be that Ailey dancer, I had mastered the plan.

The plan was simple. I had to do ballet, every day. The more I could do it the closer I would be to achieving my dream. The plan had to be efficient, I had limited time, I was at school full time from 7am to 5pm, 6 days a week (they are very weird in the French education system, we work way too much at school). But after school I was finding the time to do maybe two ballet classes, and I added the Jazz and I added Graham. So I had to choose, I could not dance everything. So, dances like Gwo ka, the traditional dance of Guadeloupe didn't make the cut. I remember coldly scratching out the only Gwo ka class that was on my schedule, to add to that day a third ballet class. I remember strongly believing (and having understood) that dances like Gwo ka would be of no help when it would come to get the audition for the Ailey School and hopefully one day the Ailey company. And you know what; I know that sadly I was right about that.

I was a walking state of denial, there was no value, no acknowledgement for where I was from, and I just wanted to get that audition. So I left home alone, at age 18, to become a dancer with absolutely no knowledge nor acknowledgement toward my Caribbean identity and African heritage. I had been raised and nurtured in a system that gave no value nor care for the dances of the African diaspora and I wasn't taught to give it value. But I am a product of the diaspora. I was set to fly without or more accurately DESPITE OF my wings.

STAGE 3: ANGER – *FRUSTRATED OUTPOURING OF BOTTLED-UP EMOTION*

There was something I didn't share about myself from the ages of 14-18, which is that I had to diet because I didn't have the right body. When I won the first prize, I associated the two; you diet and you win. I had moved to New York and you know what, I did pretty well, for about a year and a half, and then my body rebelled against me.

There are beliefs about my body image that I had integrated since I was 14; I had to diet my way into achieving the ballet body that was demanded from me and at Ailey it was no different. If the Ailey aesthetics was at the time "blacker" than I had known so far, it definitely wasn't the blackest. There are some parts that weren't acknowledged. At school, the devotion for "The Master Ballet" kept on going. To have access to the stage you had to audition, to audition you had to be in the highest levels of ballet (minimum level 5 on 7), to be in the highest level of ballet you had to have impeccable technique (I wasn't doing so bad since my first prize at the ballet competition and my rigorous work for 4 years) but you also had to be lean, thin, lengthen, many words that pretty much meant that your Black body had to look like a ballet body. You know what? The original ballet body is a white body. So I had a problem. I'm not white; I had no way to become white, so my only possible access to success was through dieting my way to a less-Black looking body.

Talk about stakes and dramas! I was 18, I became anorexic. I just stopped eating, "the master plan". Then I had absolutely no energy (no calories) to dance, but you know what? I moved up a ballet level and was cast in two shows in just a few months!

It didn't last long before my body, this angry body, saved me from this madness; I injured myself (I needed to eat). But I'm so grateful for the Achilles tendentious that I got that lasted for about two months, and had to start treating myself properly again.

However, that's where the anger came in. My body was angry; it needed to take revenge for the starving, revenge for all these things. My body had a greater plan and a great deal of anger bottled up in it.

From the time I stopped the war on food in order to be thin, to get that ballet body, I became bulimic. My poor little dancing body was lost, I was lost, I didn't know how to properly feed myself anymore, I had unlearned one of the most basic human processes, and this body of mine had a revenge to take for all the starving. So I ate, "if you're going to eat, let's eat" but I wasn't hungry, I was angry. I ate until the inevitable happened; I lost my scholarship and was kicked out of Ailey. I was a great dancer, could have been company material one day in terms of my dancing abilities and stage presence....but I was too fat.

Just to give you some perspective, I was at that time probably thinner than I am right now ...but ...there you have it. If I wanted to reach the top, I had to understand that "the top" looked like something, and that something was definitely not me.

I can tell you that anger is a small word to describe this stage of my life. So I made a decision, I'm a survivor, we are survivors. I thought, I'm not going to have Ailey quit on me, I'm going to quit. I'd rather hate the dream than give up on the dream. But it sure felt like I had given up on me. So I refused to compromise by trying to "lose the weight" like they advised me to and therefore automatically being given my scholarship back.

So I left, I said no thank you, slammed the door behind me, I made a lot of people unhappy, and I left with my angry self and disappeared in the jungle of New York at the age of 20.

This is the most angry I've ever been in my life. I was so angry, it was eating me up inside and any occasion to dance at that time felt like I was dancing OUT of myself. It was hard.

Catherine Dénécy in *Mi-Chaud, Mi-Froid* at the Let's Dance International Frontiers 2016 Launch, New Walk Museum and Art Gallery, Leicester. Photographer Matt Cawrey.

STAGE 4: BARGAINING – *SEEKING IN VAIN FOR A WAY OUT*

You know what? I am such a lucky girl. I left Ailey in January, in August I got found. It only took me six months of being lost. I had only a month in New York left before accepting my defeat and going back to Guadeloupe to study like everybody else, when I took my last audition (I was done being rejected, if that one failed that would be it for me). I arrived in the Paul Taylor Studio to audition for the Urban Bush Women. And I got the job.

I have come to reflect on the state of mind I had when I entered that room, for that audition. I was scared, I was angry, I was wounded, but most of all I didn't know Jawole and her amazing legacy at that time. This gave me less than the 200 other women who came to audition that day. I didn't know American Black dance, I only knew of Ailey, I didn't know of American dance even, I only knew the techniques of Horton and Graham because they were taught at Ailey, but didn't even know of the choreographers behind them. I was a French Caribbean woman who had just left high school and had not been offered any education in dance. A lot of the other women that auditioned with me and then danced with me in the company, had studied Jawole at school, I was clueless!.

So yes I got the job, but I wasn't educated enough to allow the joy of the news to overcome the sorrow of the loss I had just undergone. If at the time I had had the understanding of who I was and really wanted to become as an art maker, the education to support it and the tools to reach it, becoming an Urban Bush Woman would have tied with one of the last stages of the grieving model, but I didn't have all that, so I entered at that time the stage of bargaining. I was seeking a way out of the thinking that I wasn't able to be an Ailey dancer, I wasn't yet finding a way into being a dancer.

I was hurt, I was reacting. But as I said, I am such a lucky girl! And the way out I found could not have been a better way!

As a new member of the company, I totally reshaped my dance practice. It was a total deconstruction, a real deprogramming of the medical subject of ballet I had been for 15 years. We didn't use the mirror so I could no longer clinically criticise my dancing body all day every day, I could just dance! Finally! We were allowed to "be" on stage, breathing, laughing, crying, and shouting ! My body had been seen as sick, unfit, too fat, too big, in the past, but Jawole couldn't care less about how I looked; she cared about how I DANCED.

I learnt for the very first time that I could deconstruct the hierarchy that existed in my body and mind between the dances of the African Diaspora and the dances coming out or from ballet forms. And this was the tricky part; this is where the bargaining started. I was willing to learn the new forms I didn't know (even though I was from the Caribbean I was clueless about African diasporic dances, what a shame!). But I feared UNLEARNING the aesthetics of ballet. Remember that I said it had been since a young age like a personal investment and how it was deeply rooted in my spine? I was scared to lose my money, and to actually give up on that dream of mine of being with Ailey (maybe one day, if I was a good girl).

I didn't even grasp then the extent of my luck! As Jawole didn't only teach me the way out, she made me understand that it was a path that allowed no compromise. How are you going to find yourself if you bargain yourself?

I remember that day when she explained to me that in order to achieve demanding and specific techniques like Afro Cuban, Afro Haitian and African dances, I had to stop taking ballet every day. Didn't I say my spine was on lock, straight mode? How can you achieve doing a yanvalu or a cassé like that?! I had to retrieve to the core of my approach of dance and press the reset button.

That day she saved me as it is the day I accepted after 15 years of almost daily ballet classes not to take one for at least a year. By doing so, I stopped the bargaining and dived willingly into the new chance that I was offered to reconstruct my dancing body, creative mind, and my position towards dancing as a Black woman. I could finally accept its legitimacy and its value.

STAGE 5 : DEPRESSION – *FINAL REALISATION OF THE INEVITABLE*

There started for 5 years the most amazing artistic journey. I was part of a company, of a community, that allowed me to dance in a healthy, bold, genuine way and to fully own my dancing body. I was forging my artistic intelligence and growing into not just being a skilled dancer but also becoming a choreographer and a thinker. I got to know the stage, to understand the greatness and responsibility of performing. I was finally set free and was achieving my dream. If I had been an African American woman, what I am describing would not be in the part about depression, it would have been the stage of acceptance and honouring. I was stuck on "who am I?". I am a French Caribbean woman, so I had a lot more to resolve with myself and where I was from in order to know where I was going.

To explain this to you, I have a metaphor. In the film, The Matrix, the characters are given a choice. There is the red pill and the blue pill, the red pill is the choice to face the sometimes painful truth of reality, the blue pill is the blissful comfort of ignorance.

Well, Jawole was my red pill, and my acceptance to embrace my work in her company had been the choice to gladly take the pill. I faced reality working with Urban Bush Women, now I could see I was from the diaspora. I realised I was from the diaspora and didn't know anything about it, I'd never cared about it before. The ground-breaking work Jawole was making in the US, still needed to be done in my part of the world, Guadeloupe. As I had come to celebrate who I was, I realised that I didn't really have all the elements to construct my creative identity as I had spent most of my time in Guadeloupe dancing in denial.

Every day I was surrounded by glorious African American and African women who could openly express their creativity coming from a place of knowledge and love of who they were, and I wanted, I had to do my part and allow the creative young French Caribbean woman that I could become to enter the conversation.

But it wasn't simple to understand and accept at the time and the overwhelming feeling of not belonging came over me, depression came over me as I understood that I had to go back to Guadeloupe, I had to go back home to truly be found.

I had to leave behind years of work, a community, a great job, I had to because I knew that my whole story in dance had not started the right way and that my chance to reclaim it and the courage to do it would not come often, and might never come back.

I had no plan and this decision of "retrieving" back home felt like a failure at the time, but it was inevitable. I could not possibly keep going on the path of creating as an artist with so little knowledge and respect for my origins. What was clear is that I had the duty of starting and taking part in the conversation about Caribbean Contemporary Dance, and for this I had to reboot the storyline.

It was a real poker game, I could lose everything and never dance again, but I had faith that I had met every person in my career for a reason and that if it had all come down to this decision, I had to honour it.

I pressed the reset button and I packed my bags and moved back to Guadeloupe, I was 25.

BLACK WOMEN IN DANCE STEPPING OUT OF THE BARRIERS 69

Catherine Dénécy, NYC, 2009. Photographer Crush Boone.

STAGE 6 : TESTING – *SEEKING REALISTIC SOLUTIONS*

I went home, and when I arrived I started the testing stage. After the first few months of fear and sadness and even regret (what have I done?! why did I leave New York, I must be crazy!!) I started to eagerly seek what I had come to Guadeloupe to retrieve. I did so by getting to work: I started writing and creating my very first piece as a choreographer. I founded my company to support my work and I took the time (two years) to research the solutions I desperately needed. And I did so in my dance, in my body. I was very lucky, I had learned a lot, working with UBW I had learnt independence and knowledge that there was something there. Of course I read and allowed the brilliant thinking of French Caribbean writers such as Césaire and Glissant to guide me, but I knew that most of the answers I was looking for were within me. I strongly believed that all the solutions were stored in my spine and that I just had to enter the physical, mental, emotional and geographical space where I could let the knot get undone.

I choreographed the work
"Unpeubeaucoupalafoliepasdutout" (a little, a lot, madly, not at all) between 2010 and 2012.

I used the creation and writing of this work as a catharsis. I used the work to ask the questions I desperately needed answers to, such as: What does it means to be creole? By embracing many different cultures can you lose touch with where you are from? How do you manage to organise your different influences and remain true to your identity?

In other words, in this piece I was willingly undergoing the process of creolisation. I was accepting that the place in the world I was from gave me a unique perspective on the world and ability to understand it. The changes I was letting in were very deeply rooted in my personality and I allowed them to affect the way I dressed (African Caribbean fashion is no joke), the way I ate and spoke. I started having within my habits the long due dialogue between my creole influences and my French influences. I grasped the state of being creole and started my journey of creolisation.

This process affected also my dancing body, I used the creation of this piece to articulate and define my choreographic writing. I had had the opportunity to discover that I had choreographic abilities while working with Jawole and she really supported me, like she does for all her dancers (God bless her for that!) in keeping on looking for my voice because as I remember her saying "there is something there".

So I went to look for that something. I wanted to find the articulations, the solutions, the movements behind my process of creolisation. I had been accepting many dances in my body, I had finally succeeded in reprograming myself into no longer believing that there was an hierarchy between the dances coming from ballet and the ones of the African diaspora...I believed all of that, but I had experimented it from an African American perspective, I needed to now understand it from a French Caribbean/Creole perspective and discover what it looked like.

I made a great deal of discovery and a real dance signature started coming out. My research mostly came from improvisation as I knew I had to let my spine walk the talk. After two years of patience, the soup was ready, I was ready. The work toured a lot in the Caribbean; Jamaica, Cuba, St-Lucia, Dominica, and in France and the UK. I even had the honour to present it at Let's Dance International Frontiers in 2013.

I was very proud, but I knew that it wasn't over. I was seeking answers and found real solutions to position myself as a creole creator and thinker, but this piece was like a test, a prototype. I talk about me, my journey; I was defining my container and was a little stuck on me.

I knew that my real creative freedom would arrive once I would no longer need to justify who I was and could just be it, when I would be able to use the personal in a way that allowed me to reach the universal.

It was great, but it's not the last stage. I was aware that this is catharsis, this was testing, I was wondering things about me. I was trying to express me. I know I wasn't yet at the stage of creative freedom, creative thinking where you don't have to perpetually justify who you are and why you are and why you are there. You're just there. I knew it wasn't over.

STAGE 7: ACCEPTANCE – *FINALLY FINDING THE WAY FORWARD*

Here we are, to the stage of so called acceptance. There is several ways to express this phase; I have tried to find many.

Two years ago at Let's Dance International Frontiers in 2014, the conference was entitled "Creolizing Dance in a Global Age". The findings of which were subsequently published (I was thrilled when I was asked if an image of myself from *Unpeubeaucoupalafoliepasdutout* could be included, and on the page next to Pearl Primus!) But, from this book I have been really compelled by reading the thoughts on creolisation of a fellow Guadeloupean native, Gladys M. Francis. I think it is important to quote her here:

"My creolization is a displacement, a replacement and a perpetual conquest. My identity is that of variable geographies. I am a maroon. I am forever negotiating my multiethnic differences, always looking back, understanding my spaces of non/privileges, creating new spaces of happiness and redefining myself continuously. I know the limitations of my island, I know the beauty and the ugly of my island. I do not fantasise it. And I do the same with every space my body penetrates. I have my place nowhere, without anywhere to limit me. My creolization had overwhelmed me with a thousand sorrows and a thousand joys."

(Gladys M. Francis, Creolizing Dance in a Global Age, pg. 57)

As I read those words, I was still in my testing phase, I had not yet reached peace with the tumultuous process of creolisation. I was still trying to negotiate the emotions behind the perpetual displacement and conquest. I remember envying this brilliant woman, hoping for the time where I would no longer have to prove that I am ok with being creole and just be creole. I knew that my true creative freedom had not yet been launched, that I was still in a liminal stage. I wondered what it was that I had to do to get there.

I realised that like any process of grieving implies, I needed time and faith in the process.

I had successfully rebooted my system, I had accepted to undo the programme that had been implanted in my very young mind and body. I had accepted the challenges of finding "my talk" and come to understand that it was just a matter of time before I started the walk.

I was confident that my path had been genuine enough to allow me to rebel against what didn't work for me and accept what did.

It took me about three years before thinking of making another work; I wanted to wait for the liminality to be over. I knew I would feel when the integration would be completed. It happened unconsciously, one day I started writing a new piece. I dived into it and allowed my thinking to articulate. I discovered that my creative thinking was clearer, less heavy, and more accessible. I no longer had to try to create as a French Caribbean woman; I could just do it because that is who I am. I no longer feared for leftovers of my past programme to sink in my creativity. I had left the place of anger, fear, sadness, rebellion and had peacefully changed my chaos into a new reality.

I created *"Mi-Chaud, Mi-Froid, On ne peut pas plaire à tout le monde"* (Mid-Hot, Mid-Cold, you can't please everyone and I can say that the best part about this piece was to create it. I could enjoy the perpetual risk taking, because creating is risk taking. That is why I went for this model because you can take risks only when you are healed of all your wounds. Real risks. You can go and not fear that the programme that you might have comes back and seeps inside and you realise you're dancing something that is not you. You need to take care of the unconscious and that programming, because we are all programmed in a way when we come to dance the way I did. I keep in Mi-Chaud, Mi-Froid a big space of improvisation, I think a third of the work is improvisation, the last section is all improvisation. Each time it is different, because my spine might have to say more.

For an artist, creating is like thinking, sometimes even like breathing. And you know what? I feel now that I can finally breathe.

CONCLUSION

The healthy female human dancing body that I was meant to become had started being taken away from me from the age of five, from the very first ballet class I took and the reason why I took it.

I was given a drug with no realistic way to buy more of it.

I fell in love with a lover that didn't share my zipcode.

I am the working French Caribbean dancer and choreographer standing in front of you today because I had to grieve, heal the addiction, demand a healthy relationship and be successful in doing so.

I am here because I understood and accepted that this drug would never "fix" me, that the lover that I was introduced to was not real and not mine to love.

I am here because once I finished the grieving, the real love and honouring of my Black body dancing and creating could appear, because not so long ago I realised that I didn't need to desperately look for my dealer anymore as I was finally living in a permanent high.

I have shared with you my journey and many encounters. I am thankful for every part of it and aware that nothing was right or wrong, it all depends on where you come from and who you are.

The impact that places like The Ailey School, or Urban Bush Women had on me was shaped by my education and the way I came into dancing.

Each space I entered was a teacher and gave me great gifts as they forced me to start the honest conversation about my identity that I was avoiding.

Those spaces have blessed me as they forced me to return to the root of the problem that would have kept me from reaching my optimal freedom as a creator.

Those spaces have deconstructed and reconstructed me.

I took the responsibility to define my storyline and will keep on doing so as long as I will create for, as I said, Black women in dance are born warriors and survivors.

We each have our set of barriers and possess the tools and courage to jump over them.

So I keep jumping. I jump with love and honour, I jump with force and rebellion, I jump with clumsiness and precision. Dance is my way of creating, thinking and being, so make me jump! I have now come to enjoy it.

REFERENCES

Francis, Gladys. M. *"Africa, France and the French Antilles: Beyond Négritude and Créolite in Dance" Creolizing Dance in a Global Age.* Serendipity Artists Movement Ltd. (2015)

BLACK WOMEN IN DANCE STEPPING OUT OF THE BARRIERS   73

Catherine Dénécy, Paris, 2013. Photographer Philippe Virapin.

NARRATING SPACES

Adesola Akinleye in *Passing 2: The Price of a Ticket* performed as part of Biography at the Guildhall, Leicester 2016. Photographer Lisa Gilby.

ADESOLA AKINLEYE

INTRODUCTION

I am going to be discussing creativity: creative processes from the perspective of someone who identifies as a Black, Women, Artist. Immediately I need to point out that I by no means want to suggest that there is some kind of shared creative outcome that all Black women artists demonstrate. The nature of creativity seems to be that it is inherently individual in everyone. To assume it was the same across a group of people would be contradictory to the general assumption that creativity involves uniqueness. Similarly, the notion of 'Black' and 'woman' are contested labels rather than fixed identities. So this chapter is about what happens when the spectrums of Blackness, womanhood and creativity are thought about in terms of their relationship with each other. What rhythms emerge when all three are considered at the same time. In this way the chapter is not written only for those who identify as Black women artists, it is written to look at creative processes in general. Rather than seeing a deficit model, describing what is difficult about my artistic process (because undeniably racism and sexism have an impact on my creative output), the chapter looks at how my artwork traces a journey in creative development that has been spiced and enriched by the rigour of creating work outside the support of the mainstream. For me negotiating the expectations of Blackness, womanhood and creativity have been lived lessons in what Molara Ogundipe-Leslie & Carole E. Boyce Davies call 'transformational discourses' (Ogundipe-Leslie, 1994). This is because when considered together, when lived together, they each give perspective on voice and voicelessness: how we (re)count our own lives in the bigger picture of U.S. and European hegemony. In the case of dance how the dances we manifest from our bodies, narrative the spaces we occupy.

'...reject on principle the "discrimination paradigm" which operates on the basis that discrimination is a given and that each group must therefore negotiate its way out of discrimination and prove itself worthy of serious consideration...seek to transform them [oppressive practices], move...from positions of limitation to positions of action.'

(Ogundipe-Leslie, 1994, p. xvi)

I am suggesting that in identifying, and being identified as a Black woman artist, I am writing from outside the nurturing warmth of the Western mainstream identity (Appiah, 1991). However, I am not writing in order to justify my practice; instead I see this as a means to discuss, share and visualise practices in general that do not fall into the light of the mainstream. The mainstream is constructed as a place for, and of, privilege because it gives those artists within it a licence to explore without unwarranted rationalisation for what they are doing. A mark of being outside the mainstream is that your work is constantly accepted under the provision it can be made sense of by those within the mainstream. For instance, a work I created about childhood can be accepted as legitimate when it is described as being about my experience of Black childhood (rather than just childhood in general). When the work is understood as being about Black childhood my Blackness is accounted for and the work appears to become more understandable in the mainstream. This need to negotiate stereotypes for, and explain how my identity manifests within the work I make has led to questioning assumptions and deconstructing expectations being a part of the landscape of my creative process. I am not saying questioning the validity of oneself and one's work is not something all artists do internally but as a Black woman it is something that is always present externally too. To this end I have had to make peace with uncertainty and vulnerability. Therefore, I am beginning this chapter by finding the uncertainty and vulnerability in what we assume when we talk about creativity.

EXPLAINING OURSELVES INTO THE REALITY OF OTHERS

Looking-up creativity across the internet, as a way to gather general assumptions for the word, I found a number of definitions that all involved the making of some *'thing'*; creativity manifests a product. These definitions could be summed up in this phrase from an on-line dictionary:

'Creativity: The act of turning new and imaginative ideas into reality'.

But this is not what creativity has emerged as meaning through the Black woman artist lens. From my own experience and from witnessing the process of Black female friends, creativity is very often about *navigating obstacles* rather than *manifesting ideas*. From the Black woman artist perspective, the problem with seeing creativity as producing something is that this relies on the witnessing of others. It relies on the visibility of the creation, for the creative process to be recognised as having happened. For many Black women artists, the support, and resources are not available for *'ideas to become reality'*. Or in some cases the idea becomes reality but remains invisible (to the mainstream). For many, although the Black women artist is in a creative process, they feel they are doing this in a vacuum because without the 'product' of their creativity their process is not acknowledged as existing. I have had a number of conversations with fellow Black women artists where we can describe to each other the same sense of depression stemming from this place of invisibility. An artist has to be creative, but I have found the creative energy of the Black woman artist is mediated by despondency brought about by the invisibility her work often encounters. She has to learn to be creative in a positive way even at her lowest points to avoid creating negativity as a response to the invisibility that manifest as lack of support, access to, or recognition of her work.

'A creative person has to create. It doesn't really matter what you create. If such a dancer wanted to go out and build the cactus gardens where he could, in Mexico, let him do that, but something that is creative has to go on' – attributed to Katherine Dunham,

If part of the meaning of creativity is to do with *'ideas turned to reality'*, then for the Black woman artist creativity involves visibility/invisibility also. The mechanism for visibility in the post-industrial West is naming things into reality. There is a Western post-industrial need for things to be named to be *real*. This is held over from a colonial need for *things* to be discovered and named so that they can be explained in order for them to become visible, even if the naming is under a complete misapprehension of what the *thing* is (Gould, 1996; Smith, 1999). Those *things* that are unnamed remain invisible. From this Western dualist perspective of certainty, something must be categorised and named to be addressed as *real* (Dewey & Boydston, 2008). The problem is that this naming ceremony goes on within the mainstream constructs for art work and as I have suggested my Black female identity sits outside this. My visibility as an artist then relies on the imagination and ability of the mainstream to comprehend and name my work. So much of the success of my work has relied on my growing ability to explain my artistry into visibility. However, there are *things* about my work that are un-nameable within the mainstream because they originate from, and refer to, life outside the mainstream. Those elements of the work remain unnamed and therefore often invisible.

If creativity is about turning *'ideas into reality'*, then for the Black women artists that reality is restricted by the limits of the imagination of the mainstream. What I can become as a visible artist is limited by what people can imagine me and my work becoming. I am limited by how well I can be named and seen. This is the frustration inherent in so many conversations I have had with fellow Black women artists. But our experiences of invisibility and imagination can be used to interrogate what creativity can be. We can move away from creativity as the turning of *'new ideas into reality'*, to seeing creativity as the act of freeing ourselves from the constraints of our imaginations, and freeing ourselves from what is imagined for us.

THE WAGES OF INVISIBILITY COULD BE THE RICHES OF CREATIVITY

As an artist I am all the relationships and rhythms in my life (Mahina, 2004). I don't want to be nameable because I come from a personal cultural background that values between-ness, transformation, movement; not fixed *things*. I am not *normal*. My Blackness, my womanhood, and my artistry often mean I am cast as *other* in the places I call home. But in embracing who I feel I am, I am willing to pay the price of *otherness*. However, as I have discussed above the ambiguity of being *other*, (not being nameable) brings with it an invisibility. Invisibility are the wages of being 'other'. But rather than knocking on the door of acceptance I think it is important to notice that as Black women artists, we have something to say and something to create that is always universal because invisibility is a disease across genders, assignments, ages, cultures, and geographic locations.

I am not forgetting the depression and demoralisation so many of us feel at points in our careers. The imposition of invisibility is in the limitation of what we can envisage ourselves creating. But more deeply affected by invisibility are the narratives we allow ourselves to *real*-ise – how we narrate the possibility of the spaces we occupy, how we narrate our creative lives. I am not suggesting we should strive to avoid the mainstream if we wish to be there but I am saying we need to recognise it takes a toll on our creative energy. And we need to help each other replenish from this. I am suggesting that not too much creative energy be spent explaining ourselves into the reality of the mainstream in order to be visible. Instead we can use our notion of creativity *(freeing ourselves from what is imagined for us)* to fuel seeing ourselves for ourselves. The Black woman artist must see herself –must be her own witness to her own creative process, even when nobody else will witness it with her. I feel this attitude is important for all those involved in creativity, but Black women artists lead the way in this because surviving as a Black woman artist so often requires the *truth* in finding a place of being the lone witness to your own creative process.

I began my pilgrimage to this place when I created the work *Truth & Transparency*, 2005 (working title: *Climbing with bare feet*). This work was inspired by Ralph Ellison's novel *Invisible Man* (Ellison, 2001). I created a dance piece for two men. Across Ellison's novel the word *light can be read as a metaphor for the 'Western mainstream' or US and European* hegemony. The man in the novel is looking for light and at the end of the book he is living in the darkness of a basement using light he gets from tapping into other people's power systems (Ellison, 2001).

"Maybe it is exactly because I am invisible. Light confirms my reality, gives birth to my form...Without light I am not only invisible, but formless as well..."

(Ellison, 2001, pp. 6-7)

Using this metaphor of light for the Western mainstream, Ellison raises questions for me about the privileged observer of art to whom we must narrate ourselves into visibility: explaining ourselves into the light. As a Black woman artist Ellison's words resonate with me, '*I am invisible and light confirms my reality*'. I feel the affirmation the character in the novel makes, '...*without light I am not only invisible, but formless as well...*', is Ellison sounding a warning against allowing yourself to only be defined by others. Exploring during my choreographic process for this work I found that for light to exist it needs an object (a named thing). Light is only noticed as present through the objects it highlights, and through its absence elsewhere. For the piece *Truth & Transparency* I choreographed, exploring how the dance could rely on darkness to be clear rather than light. Rather than making a work that relied on light I looked at how I could make work that relied on dark. I recontextulised my work in terms of dark instead of light. I used projection which requires darkness for clarity to create the spaces on stage. Using projection on stage I created a space where dancers could only be seen in the shadow of the interrupted light of the projection. I used white-outs rather than black-outs at moments of change in the work. Part of the creative process of the work was my consideration of the exchange of power between visibility and light; and what is lost in the dance as we attempt to be recognised in the *light*. Physically I explored how light helps with vision but it is not vision. The work explores a 'dialogue between light and consciousness' (Olafur, Tuyl, & Broeker, 2004) how dance becomes visible on the stage.

Researching for Truth & Transparency I explored the work of light-artist Olafur Eliasson. I looked at relationships between light, vision and (in)visibility.

"...*vision became relocated in the subjectivity of the observer, two intertwined paths opened up. One led out towards all the multiple affirmations of the sovereignty and autonomy of vision derived from the newly empowered body...*"

(Olafur et al., 2004, p. 31)

The physical re-positioning of light in the choreographic space and process of the work developed my artistic practice philosophically also. In order to engage in my vision, to be visible to myself, to give myself form, my '*newly empowered body*' is one that feels comfortable in its creative truth - there is much of me I cannot, or does not want to be, explained in words or in light. I found how my creative self *feels* in the dark. During the choreographic process for *Truth & Transparency* I needed to find how I create a canvas/container/situation/process for this dark, how it felt sensing to happen.. I can trace my use of projection in my dance work back to the creative exploration I did with the making of *Truth & Transparency*. But as with the piece, the beauty and artistry is in the dance itself, of which the projected light is just one of the relationships that manifests within the art.

As part of my art practice I now constantly reflect on my construction of my relationships with light and dark. This reflection manifests itself even within small details of day-to-day life, for instance my notebooks are black pages on which I write with light ink. I don't use the embodied metaphor of dark being bad ('The film was scary and dark'), and light being easier ('I'm feeling light because I finished my exams'). These are physical, felt metaphors (Lakoff & Johnson, 1980) and I work in the physical, felt medium of dance so I will not adopt them for understanding my lived experiences. This is to give myself a manifesto for healing invisibility within my own creative process. This is to acknowledge that as I am identified as a Black woman artist I need to claim my own relationship with Blackness. I am not a Black woman artist because of how I am (un)seen. This is about seeing myself; 'autonomy of vision'– not to need the light in order to be visible to myself.

Rose's Jingle Dress. Photographer Barry Lewis.

CREATIVE SUCCESS IS A PLACE OF BRAVERY.

The expectation of the racist and colonial gaze (Hooks, 1992; Johnson, 2003) is that the Black artist's work is to clarify Blackness. But creativity demands we make from within. I create from *within* my Blackness, not to explain it to someone else. I also create from *within* my identity as a woman, as trans-national Nigerian British, as working class, as a mother, as the daughter of a white woman, as Indigenous, as a dyslexic, as a dancer.

Five years on from 2005, in 2010, creating from within my Black womanhood rather that to explain it I choreographed the work *Rose's Jingle Dress* (working title: *The Jingle Dress*) for young audiences. From my own growing family and from working with young people from African and Indigenous backgrounds I had started to be moved by seeing the invisibility of their experiences in contemporary contexts (particularly contemporary dance contexts). To be not mainstream is often constructed as to be of the *past*. Indigenous peoples are often talked about in past tense as if 'they' did not even exist today. African aesthetics are engaged with as comments on nostalgic post-industrial values at worst, and an internal look at post-colonialism recovery at best, but rarely as a contemporary commentary on 21st century global 'realities' (Appiah, 1991). I created *Rose's Jingle Dress* to celebrate the birth of a Lakota friend's first child (see Akinleye. A, *Rose's Jingle Dress: Cultural Legacies and Contemporary Contexts in Indigenous Health & Art edited collection*, forthcoming). Without realising it in *Rose's Jingle Dress* I challenged whose narratives contemporary dance could be about. By making a contemporary dance work from Black and Indigenous perspectives for the non-mainstream audience of children I had some how unconsciously sidestepped the mainstream altogether.

Although the work was well received I was also asked on a number of occasions how as a Black woman I could justify the topic of the piece. *Rose's Jingle Dress* marked the beginning of my creating work that spoke of, for, and about narratives not within the context of the mainstream, or as a response to the mainstream, but from the *dark, felt place* of my own starting point and interactions. Creativity, as I have defined it above, the *act of freeing ourselves from the constraints of our imaginations* allows us to value the development of a relationship with creativity processes in which we become more visible to ourselves, we begin to witness our own creative process regardless of visibility of output. We respond to our lived experiences from within our own darkness. I think that in order to move into the creativity of *beyond your own imagination* we need to start in the darkness of our unknown. A place where you feel, sense, and collaborate. This is not a place of light; it is a place of bravery.

EPISTEMOLOGY OF RESISTANCE: CREATIVITY INVOLVES GIVING YOURSELF TIME FOR PROCESS

My last interrogation of creativity in relation to what happens when the spectrums of Blackness, womanhood and creativity are thought about together, is to look at the currency of time in the creative process. Another 5 years on, 2015, and I had been able to establish my creative process quite clearly for myself. Creativity needs time for process. It is the time for process that is so protected by the privileged of the mainstream. Creative process requires money, most importantly it requires a nurturing gaze that has the time to wait for creativity to emerge. It is enormously important to have a relationship with your creative process because it is trusting you have a process that allows you the time to wander in the dark softness of the unknown without feeling you will become smothered or lost. Trusting the time of process grounds you.

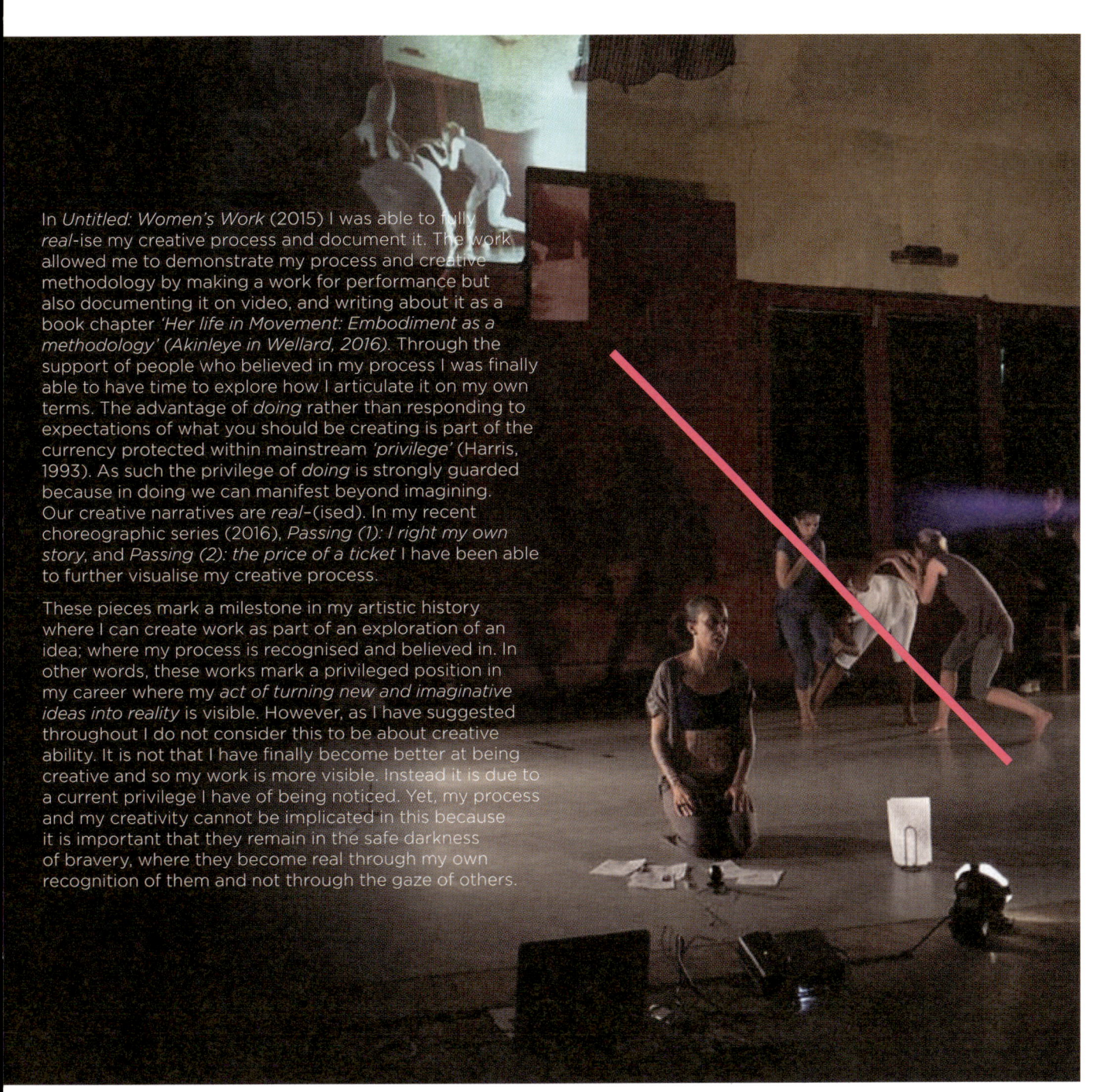

In *Untitled: Women's Work* (2015) I was able to fully *real*-ise my creative process and document it. The work allowed me to demonstrate my process and creative methodology by making a work for performance but also documenting it on video, and writing about it as a book chapter *'Her life in Movement: Embodiment as a methodology' (Akinleye in Wellard, 2016)*. Through the support of people who believed in my process I was finally able to have time to explore how I articulate it on my own terms. The advantage of *doing* rather than responding to expectations of what you should be creating is part of the currency protected within mainstream *'privilege'* (Harris, 1993). As such the privilege of *doing* is strongly guarded because in doing we can manifest beyond imagining. Our creative narratives are *real*-(ised). In my recent choreographic series (2016), *Passing (1): I right my own story*, and *Passing (2): the price of a ticket* I have been able to further visualise my creative process.

These pieces mark a milestone in my artistic history where I can create work as part of an exploration of an idea; where my process is recognised and believed in. In other words, these works mark a privileged position in my career where my *act of turning new and imaginative ideas into reality* is visible. However, as I have suggested throughout I do not consider this to be about creative ability. It is not that I have finally become better at being creative and so my work is more visible. Instead it is due to a current privilege I have of being noticed. Yet, my process and my creativity cannot be implicated in this because it is important that they remain in the safe darkness of bravery, where they become real through my own recognition of them and not through the gaze of others.

Passing 1. I right my own story. Photographer Scott Lipiec.

82 · **BLACK WOMEN IN DANCE** STEPPING OUT OF THE BARRIERS

Untitled Womens Work. Photographer Barry Lewis.

CONCLUSION

What happens when the spectrums of Blackness, womanhood and creativity are thought about in terms of their relationship with each other is a multi-layered noticing of creativity as a physical, philosophical and responsive experience. The landscape of which involves freeing ourselves from the constraints of our imaginations, and freeing ourselves from what is imagined for us. Creativity appears then as a transformational process that is in part about challenging the discourses we perceive as shaping who we are. Highlighted for me by my own Blackness and womanhood, I feel the creative process is universally informed by a sense of *resilient navigation* rather than a sense of *producing*. The rhythms that are created by my Black, female identities narrates the spaces I occupy as an artist. The rigour or difficulty of balancing these identities with mainstream expectations of what they mean requires a creative strength and resilience. The strength and resilience of creativity has been bravely exemplified for me through knowing and working with inspirational artists, who identify as being Black and Indigenous women and who have a persistent need to have an authentic voice in their own creative practices.

With love to Gloria, Leonora, Brenda, Hopal, Pawlet, Amy and Sandra.

REFERENCES

Appiah, K. (1991). Is the Post in Postmodernism the Post in Postcolonial? *Critcal Inquiry, 17*(2), 336-357.

Dewey, J., & Boydston, J. A. (2008). *The later works of John Dewey, 1925-1953* (Vol. 4: The Quest for Certainty). Carbondale: Southern Illinois University Press.

Ellison, R. (2001). *Invisible man*. London: Penguin.

Gould, S. J. (1996). *The mismeasure of man* (Rev. and expanded. ed.). New York ; London: Norton.

Hooks, B. (1992). *Black looks : race and representation*. Boston, MA: South End Press.

Johnson, E. P. (2003). *Appropriating blackness : performance and the politics of authenticity*. Durham, N.C. ; London: Duke University Press.

Lakoff, G., & Johnson, M. (1980). *Metaphors we live by*. Chicago: University of Chicago Press.

Mahina, O. (2004). *Art as ta-va 'Time-Space' transformation*. Auckland, New Zealand: Center for Pacific Studies, University of Auckland.

Ogundipe-Leslie, M. (1994). *Re-creating ourselves : African women & critical transformations*. Trenton, N.J.: Africa World Press.

Olafur, E., Tuyl, G. v., & Broeker, H. (2004). *Olafur Eliasson : your lighthouse : works with light 1991-2004*. Ostfilden-Ruit: Hatje Cantz Verlag.

Smith, L. T. (1999). *Decolonizing methodologies : research and indigenous peoples*. London ; New York, Dunedin, N.Z., New York: Zed Books; University of Otago Press; Distributed in the USA exclusively by St. Martin's Press.

Wellard, I. e. (2016). *Researching embodied sport : exploring movement cultures*.

THE GREY AREA

Jessica Walker. Photographer Karen King.

JESSICA WALKER

My chapter in this necessary publication considers the presence of another societal group that exists within the category of "Black": the "Mixed Race" individual. The population of racially mixed persons in our contemporary age grew by 75% in the 1990s and became the fastest growing minority in Great Britain. This provides a valid vehicle for examining Mixed Race[1] identity in the British dance industry and in choreographic practice.

ME, MYSELF AND WHY

As a woman who is of both Jamaican and German parentage, I was very aware from a young age of my dislocation in society. I understood that I was walking in two worlds and still somehow belonging in neither, being the Oreo throughout school and the "lighty" at university. Whilst choreography as a career found me, I wanted to understand my place within its industry: what is important about my background and what significance may I bring where the issues of the "Mixed Race" experience is different to that of the "Black" but simultaneously contributes to its discourse of social policy in our contemporary dance industry.

Mixed Race choreographer Alexandrina Hemsley stated in interview that 'We [...] don't see ourselves in the media, in parliament, on stage, on soap operas and this is a huge problem when not only trying to make work and narratives around Mixed Race experiences more visible but also when wanting to become a self-confident and self-aware citizen' (Hemsley 2015). Hemsley's comment caused me to consider the place of the Mixed Race choreographer and the lack of discourse around the experience of being Mixed Race within the dance world. A "Mixed Race tradition", not a past but a precedent, and a way of making dance that relates to its issues, is yet to be realised.

MY OBSERVATIONS

For my university dissertation I investigated the works of three British Mixed Race choreographers, Alesandra Seutin, Alexandrina Hemsley and Henri Oguike. Through examining what they said about their works and the discourse of Mixed Race identity, my study acted as a metadiscourse that both drew attention to the significance of the works of choreographers from the background and unique experience of being 'between two worlds'[2] and questions the necessity for further Mixed Race discourse in the contemporary British dance arena.

Despite the choreographers in discussion having the shared experience of being of Black-White parentage, there is a complex spectrum in how their choreographies manifest themselves and I discovered very quickly that their approaches to handling the topic of their identity were incredibly varied. Whilst Alesandra Seutin of Belgian and Zimbabwean descent uses her work as a device to encourage discussion about Mixed Race identity, Alexandrina Hemsley (who collaborates with Black choreographer Jamila Johnson-Small as *Project O*) uses unforgiving and unsettling subversions of stereotypes to confront the mainstays of being a Mixed Race woman. At the other end of the spectrum is Henri Oguike, a mainstream choreographer of Welsh and Nigerian descent whose approaches to identity politics in his choreographic practice appear to be non-existent. Due to the fluidity in ethnic self-identification (where Mixed Race individuals are able to identify as being Black, White, both or even neither [Tizard & Phoenix 2001, p. 223] some individuals are proud to carry their Mixed Race identity, whilst others may feel burdened by the responsibility of the label (Freakley 1998).

[1] Although the term is both vague and problematic, "Mixed Race" is widely used to describe individuals who have one white European and one Black African-Caribbean parent. I use the term in this study as it is a label that I (for now) self-identify with and accept as a result of my research. I write the words with capitals as I intend to give it authority before "mediocritising" (Paul 2012) a group of people with such a vague definition.

[2] As sung by Nina Simone in 1966.

Jessica Walker in *Tick the Box (Mixed Other)* performed as part of *Biography* at the Guildhall, Leicester 2016. Photographer Matt Cawrey.

Whilst Seutin not only self-identifies as a Mixed Race citizen, she uses her work as a device for negotiating racial ambiguity with the public. Hemsley stated that as a Mixed Race individual she experiences life as "other" to the predominant white heterosexual male narrative, and unwittingly appropriates the term 'queer' as a way to express her otherness (Hemsley 2015). Alternatively, Oguike preferred to identify solely as a Welshman upon entering the dance industry at London Contemporary Dance School (Adewole 2016). Since then, his works have stuck closely to the Western contemporary dance aesthetic atavistic of modern dance and contemporary ballet. When interviewed, he is firm in the notion that his Mixed Race heritage does not influence his work, stating 'it's not until it is highlighted that I become aware of being mixed' (Oguike 2015). Oguike's identification is in line with what Donovan Chamberlayne describes as an 'I amism: I am not "black" or "white", I am just me?' (Chamberlayne 1996, p. xx).

As dual-hybridity has become a reflexive moral battleground in recent years due to differing modes of self-identification and engagement in the discourse, it is currently inappropriate to typify the works of Mixed Race choreographers solely based on their ancestry. Notwithstanding, there are identifiable similarities in the movement choices within their choreographic works that are resonant of diasporic aesthetic. Whilst Seutin makes use of Germaine Acogny technique[3] in order to present Africanist aesthetic as a meaningful device for movement exploration and demonstration of Mixed Race narrative, Hemsley and Johnson-Small use subtle African Caribbean hip and shoulder gyrations in order to subvert the history, complexity and meaningfulness of the Black social dance. Oguike's choreographies have often been noted for not being representative of his Nigerian heritage with the "tigritude"[4] evidenced with other choreographers. Although 'he resists branding himself as some exotic blend of street and classic, African and British' (Mackrell 2006), there is observable evidence of Africanist sensibility in Oguike's work. One example is evident in his 2009 choreography *Treading Softly* in which Oguike gave Schubert's quartet 'a muscular heft [with] African-inflected language' (Mackrell 2009). Similarly, *Four Seasons* sees the dancers' 'pelvises grind as each clasps hands overhead, a victoriously sexual move rendered crude through repetition' (Hutera 2013, p. 10). Brenda Dixon Gottschild states in her 1993 publication Digging The Africanist Presence that 'the Africanist aesthetic values repetition or, more precisely, repetition as intensification' (Dixon Gottschild 1998, p. 8). This reveals Oguike's use of repetition in *Four Seasons* is having the same effect used within African culture to reiterate or clarify an idea.

Although the choreographers' use of Africanist aesthetic and hybridity create a dialogue between cultures that both negotiates and devises a mutual and complimentary co-existence, one cannot use hybridity to identify the Mixed Race identity in choreography. This is due to choreographers outside the racial category of Mixed Race also employing choreographic hybridisation, such as recognised choreographers Akram Khan and Bawren Tavaziva. These, however, are examples of cultural aesthetic hybridisation where 'the diasporised meets the host in the scene of migration' (Hutnyk 2005, p. 79). This holds a different narrative to those of Mixed Race choreographers, who are the children and grandchildren of the diasporised and experience an upbringing with two cultures as a product of genetic hybridisation. Mixed Race choreo-dancer Greta Mendez discusses her hybridised dance style as such: 'I have a cross between a classical and a contemporary training, so anything I do is a symbiosis of all those things' (Mendez 2007, p. 38).

[3] A codified contemporary African dance style that is based on traditional Senegalese movement and the techniques of Classical ballet, release and Graham.
[4] A colloquial term coined by novelist Wole Soyinka that expresses the 'approaches adopted by Negritude in creating awareness about the African man's heritage and in asserting negritude' (Ariole 2013, p. 5).

Mendez asserts that her dance work is a result of the dance styles experienced before that of her skin colour or ethnic ancestry, and that blood quantums should not be used to define identity before that of lived experience (Durrow 2015). Unfortunately, society often pressures Mixed Race individuals to choose just one race due to outdated use of hypodescent, otherwise known as the "one-drop rule". This prescribes that individuals with mixed heritage of any kind between differing socio-economic or ethnic groups are assigned to the subordinate group. This trend occurs within the dance industry and is experienced by Mixed Race choreographers as the term "Black dance" extends to those with dual heritage, negating the white half of their ancestral identity. Tharp enlightened me to this fact in Serendiptiy's 2013 publication *Hidden Movement*, where he commented on this tension within the dance industry's demography, stating 'I start to rebel the moment someone tries to put a label on me, especially when it's one that appears to negate one half of my identity. I've been labelled as a Black choreographer and a Black dancer - but never a white one' (Tharp 2013, p. 21). This identifies that critics often see the race, and/or the skin colour, of the dancer before the dance itself. Seutin's choreography *Ceci N'est Pas Noire!* premiered in 2013 and actively confronts the issue of hypodescent in our modern day society. The title itself makes reference to the 1929 surrealist painting *The Treachery of Images: Ceci n'est pas une pipe* by René Magritte, indicating that the work will challenge audiences to reconsider the authority of socially constructed labels. Like Magritte, Seutin invites viewers to reconsider approaches to identity perception whilst informing that skin colour is not an appropriate signifier of one's ethnic, biological or personal identity or artistic work.

The extent at which there is a Mixed Race "tradition" is still relatively un-measurable due to the very little literature about Mixed Race choreographers. As this precedent for the Mixed Race identity in the British dance industry is apparently non-existent, the choreographers in discussion will be the first group of recognised contemporary dance artists of Mixed Race descent in the UK. Contributor of *The New York Times* stated that 'It is important for us [Mixed Race citizens] to negotiate racial identities that reflect our heritage, culture and experience, which includes how we are perceived by others' (Erekson 2015). Further discourse on Mixed Race identity in the British dance industry will permit the formulation of new strategies that may give consideration to the increasingly prevalent Mixed Race identity in performance and in the classification of one's identity and artistry.

HOW AM I CONTRIBUTING?

It was not until 2015 that I myself began to use my work to contribute to a Mixed Race discourse. This was due to the fact that I was not previously affluent in its politics, although I had felt its pull. By examining the works of these choreographers during my study, I was able to start the lifelong investigation of my own place within the dance industry and how I can and am able to contribute to its politics.

Whilst I was classically trained in Ballet and was also highly capable in Jazz and Tap, I discovered African movement upon watching Bawren Tavaziva's *Sensual Africa*. As a result I took myself into London after school in order to train in African Contemporary dance at The Place with Akosua Boakye, who then became my long-term mentor. Through African Contemporary dance I found a rhythm and ferocity that my body agreed with; a style that shared the architectural values evident in Ballet and the more grounded aesthetic of African dance. However, as I have grown older and developed my practice, my movement has become continually interlaced with subtle expression and/or stoicism that makes complex works in a manner similarly seen in German Expressionist dance.

In a similar fashion to Henri Oguike, not all of my works have confronted racial identity politics. In February 2016 I choreographed *Exit Eve*, a dance piece for screen commissioned by Random Acts for national broadcasting on Channel 4. Set in a nightclub with four expressionless female dancers dressed in frocks and heels, the work explored interpersonal relationships amongst the modern everywoman; the ally, the opponent and the paramour. This was my own personal version of dv8's *Enter Achilles* turned on its head with champagne and flashing knickers. Whilst *Exit Eve* did not discuss the issues of Mixed Race identity, the observable race in the piece was a major consideration for me. I wanted to ensure that there was an evident ethnic mix in order to discuss the modern everywoman to avoid isolating or making social commentary any one or two ethnic groups. These considerations in my work proved that as my own theoretical study progressed I was becoming more aware of the ways in which audiences and critics understand dance works, and how racial equality, be it in my own practice or in the media, impacts subsequent interpretations: will people classify my work as Black dance? Will I be more successful if I make "Black work" to please audiences? I began to feel uncomfortable with the notion of a whole half of my European identity being disregarded in a similar manner to Kenneth Tharp.

My developing work *Grey Baby*, a section of which I performed at the Black Women In Dance: Stepping Out of the Barriers conference, actively confronts my concerns of binary categorisation and Westernised stereotyping. I named the section *Tick the Box: Mixed/Other*, and it is an adaptation of Sidi Larbi Cherkaoui's *Faun* and has its roots in Nijinsky's 1912 production *L'après midi d'un faune*. Upon further research I came to understand that it was an exploration of being between the two states of man and animal, and this held great resonance resonated for me as I too felt that condition. In order to discuss the matter through movement, I combined African-Caribbean and Western movement aesthetics and cross-layered this with phrases of success and failure portrayed through my vertical height within the space. This generated a particular rhythm for the piece, negating the need for aural accompaniment as the sound of my movement and my exasperated breath successfully enhanced the concept of internal struggle. I perform the work in a flesh-toned leotard, removing me from any societal influences and exposing my body in a similar way to a newborn. Through this I place myself prone in the performance space before an audience who I feel inflicted to please. Urban Bush Women's founder Jawole Willa Jo Zollar saw the piece performed twice, and informed me that it presented an authentic sense of vulnerability and dis-location. Other audience members questioned whether I was performing a "Mixed Race" style of movement, and whilst they did not fall into the trap of binary categorisation, it informed me that interpretation is still relative to the societal state in which it is made. This means that whilst views towards Mixed Race individuals and its choreographers may be shifting, there is still a need for further research into how meaning is expressed in choreographic practice and what that signifies for the fluid social structures of the British dance demographic.

Grey Baby is developing to confront the issues regarding stereotyping and the effects of essentialism through playful and insightful devices. The full-length work will be performed at Serendipity's Autograph event, and I look forward to getting further feedback in order to develop my theoretical and choreographic practice further.

CONCLUSION

News of the Mixed Race experience is slowly emerging in advocacy organisations, websites and literature and the social issues being brought to light are shared experiences of choreographers of this racial group. My dissertation taught me that it is not non-whiteness that is a common thematic in the discourse of Mixed Race individuals, but is instead the 'ideological preconceptions of "self" and "other"' (Hallam & Street 2000, p. 6) and their re-establishment as secure and non-ambiguous beings through the white gaze.

For the sake of the anticipated increase of Mixed Race people over the next fifty years, the British dance sector may shift from its pragmatic methods of socially structuring the sector through further discourse on the Mixed Race presence, and have a more contemporary dance society that reflects the current post-postmodern social climate of the UK.

REFERENCES

Adewole, F. (2016) [Interview with Jessica Walker, 06/04/2016].

Ariole, V. C. (2013) *Negritude And Tigritude: An Analysis Of Language Contents For Development Purposes*. Lagos, University of Lagos. [online]. Available from: https://submissions.scholasticahq.com/api/v1/attachments/339/download [accessed 07/04/2016].

Chamberlayne, D. (1996) In: Ifekwunigwe, J. O. (2004) *Mixed Race Studies*. London, Routledge.

Dixon Gottschild, B. (1998) *Digging The Africanist Presence In American Performance: Dance And Other Contexts*. London, Praeger.

Durrow, H. W. (2015) Identity, Race or Otherwise, Is Your Lived Experience. In: *The New York Times* [online]. Available from: http://www.nytimes.com/roomfordebate/2015/06/16/how-fluid-is-racial-identity/identity-race-or-otherwise-is-your-lived-experience [accessed 04/04/2016].

Erekson, A. K. (2015) Being Able to Negotiate Our Racial Identity is Important. In: *The New York Times* [online]. Available from: http://www.nytimes.com/roomfordebate/2015/06/16/how-fluid-is-racial-identity/being-able-to-negotiate-our-racial-identity-is-important [accessed 08/04/2016].

Freakley, V. (1998) The Realisation of Who I Am. In: *Animated* [online]. Available from: http://www.communitydance.org.uk/DB/animated-library/the-realisation-of-who-i-am.html?ed=14052 [accessed 11/11/2015].

Hallam, E. and Street, B. V. (2000) *Cultural Encounters: Representing Otherness*. Abingdon, Routledge.

Hemsley, A. (2015) In: HUDSON, R. (2015) Project O: The Dance Industry Is Racist Too. *Voice Online* [online]. Available from: http://www.voice-online.co.uk/article/project-o-dance-industry-racist-too [accessed 11/12/2015].

Hutera, D. (2013) Dance. In: *The Times* (February 14), p. 10.

Hutnyk, J. (2005) Hybridity. In: *Ethnic and Racial Studies*. 28 (1), pp. 79-102.

Mackrell, J. (2006) Keep On Moving. In: *The Guardian* [online]. Available from: http://www.theguardian.com/stage/2006/feb/16/dance [accessed 20/12/2015].

Mackrell, J. (2009) Rambert Dance Company. In: *The Guardian* [online]. Available from: http://www.theguardian.com/stage/2009/nov/04/rambert-dance-company-review [accessed 02/02/2016].

Mendez, G. In: Brooks, J. (2007) Mass Mover: Interview with Greta Mendez. In: ADEWOLE, F. (2007) *Voicing Black Dance*. London, The Association of Dance of the African Diaspora, pp. 32-44.

Oguike, H. (2015) In: Raimi-Abraham, F. (2014) Zaynnah Conversation With Henri Oguike. In: *Zaynnah Magazine* [online]. Available from: http://zaynnahmagazine.blogspot.co.uk/2015/09/zaynnah-conversationwith-henri-oguike.html [accessed 02/04/2016].

Paul, A. L. (2012) Recollections of the Asia-Pacific International Dance Conference. In: *Theatre of Rhythm and Dance* [online]. Available from: http://www.annalouisepaul.com.au/blog/index.php/2012/01/26/recollections-of-the-asia-pacific-international-dance-conference-22-25-september-2011/ [accessed 02/04/2016].

Tharp, K. O. (2013) Do We Need This Term Black Dance? In: *Hidden Movement: Contemporary Voices of Black British Dance*. Leicester, Serendipity Arts Movement, pp. 17-25.

Tizard, B. and Phoenix, A. (2002) *Black, White or Mixed Race? Race and racism in the lives of young people of mixed parentage*. London, Routledge.

Vest, J. L. (2016). Being and Not Being, Knowing and Not Knowing. In: BOTTS, T. F. (2016) *Philosophy and the Mixed Race Experience*. Maryland, Lexington Books, pp. 93-117.

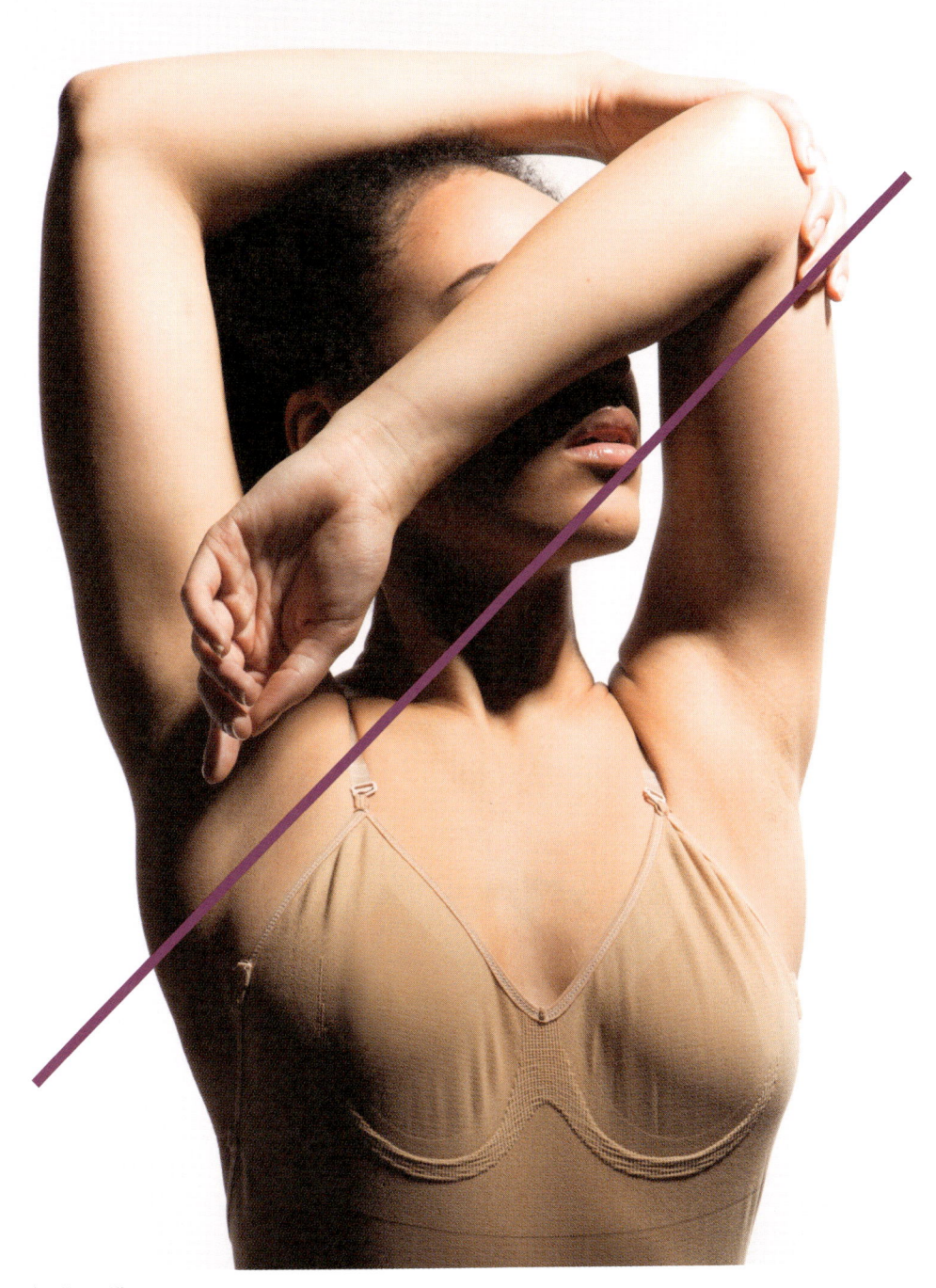

BLACK WOMEN IN DANCE STEPPING OUT OF THE BARRIERS

Jessica Walker. Photographer Karen King.

MY DUALITY, MY STRENGTH

Stephen Derrick and Sharon Watson in *Covering Ground*, choreographed by Shapiro and Smith, 1994. Photographer Steve Hanson/Phoenix Dance Theatre.

SHARON WATSON

For this publication, I was asked to explore the role that dance companies play in supporting Black dancers and choreographers. I have a story in terms of my personal journey to share. The journey I have made is quite an interesting one. I don't make work that is labelled Black or White, and I don't make work that is seen or meant for specific audiences. I make work because I enjoy the subject matter as something I want to learn about and something I want to share. If I look back then the question "What do we choose to see and what do we choose to acknowledge?" becomes really key in terms of my journey, and a question to keep in mind throughout this paper.

JOINING PHOENIX AS A DANCER

I was one of the first women to join Phoenix Dance Theatre (or as it was known at the time, Phoenix Dance Company) in 1989. I was invited, but this wasn't a given, I had to earn my place. What was interesting during that period of time is that I wasn't on my own in terms of taking that journey forward. There were four of us in total, a very small number of Black females that had the opportunity to begin to change history in the way that we understood it at the time; myself with three other pioneers of contemporary dance, with Pam Johnson, alongside Seline Thomas and my sister Dawn Donaldson. A very conservative number, but a new pioneering and motion in dance, carrying with it responsibilities that at the time perhaps weren't as clear to us moving through this journey, but reflecting back have become very important. Some years later, I was made to understand that actually I wasn't going to be invited to join the company. But looking back, I remember my sister was on the phone saying "Sharon, I'm on my way, getting ready to go to Leeds, it's happening!" I responded, "What do you mean it's happening?" The question of choice regarding which women should be part of the organisation was a big debate. I was already forging ahead building a career in London, one that was considered successful to date, so I understand why there was some concern as to whether I should be taken away from this and put into a process where the outcome was unknown. But I'm glad someone saw sense in my opinion and I was able to join the other women, all very powerful voices and very articulate on what they had to contribute to this new opportunity. We were entering a challenging process with little knowledge as to how this would play out.

So a new chapter started. The Tuckman theory of "forming, storming, norming and performing" was beginning to kick in, however we realised quite early on that this process wasn't just going to happen over the initial six-month period that we were contracted to be with the company. This process was a cycle that would continue well into the future, through the many years that we were engaged with the company that had started out as all Black, all male. The forming was a decision that wasn't part of our decision making, but made by an artistic director that felt it was time for change.

In hindsight, change that was timely, change that was inevitable and wasn't plain sailing, adding four very strong vocal women to a group of very powerful Black men. A lot of the debates and conversations in that early forming and storming stage took a long time for us to find any kind of grounding. The storming was not just about the fact that we had the opportunity to perform, that we could engage and actually begin to change the status quo! We clearly identified this opportunity to see how we could extend ourselves and our voices above and beyond expectation. So the storming process was ongoing, with no real conclusion in sight. It was taking weeks, in fact months, to go through the forming, storming, norming, performing scenario. In hindsight I guess what we were experiencing was an igniting of passion taking shape in and out of the studio. Slowly, the labels began to fall into place about who we were and how we were moving forward. But I do recall conversations where I think the voices of the women started to become a lot more powerful than the voices of the men.

Our working environment at times became volatile, there was no shortage of passion knowing we were coming from slightly different places of development, and that resonated more and more. In saying that, we knew the men, we grew up with them. We went to school with a lot of them, we went to church with some of them, went through vocational training with some of them and some developed personal relationships. However, there was something about this territorial place that had been, up to this point, exclusively men only, and was now being occupied by women; women that had moved away from Leeds and returned having taken on new experiences, feeling strongly that we were performers first and foremost and that we were not Black dancers! Collectively not quite knowing how much ownership of this we should embrace? The uncertainty was felt by us all! But actually we weren't denying it; we just felt we wanted to be on an equal footing, a level-playing field. So the voices once again began to resonate a lot stronger in terms of identity, one that would allow us to be who we are as performers, as people, as opposed to taking on a colour identity to define who we are and what we're about to do.

The work within the organisation at the time really was not talking about the Black culture, it wasn't about trying to differentiate ourselves as Black people, it was about the work. It was about artists wanting to create something that was passionate to them, for them, about them; work that connected emotionally and physically. A lot of us were first generation British Black. Our first experience of dance was through a contemporary experience, the Graham technique being our first introduction to dance followed by classical ballet, jazz, hip hop, and everything else in between. But that wasn't the driver.

Contemporary dance as we knew it, was about a form of expression, wherever that came from. We sensed a barrier in terms of us wanting to move that form forward. For some it wasn't enough to have the work branded contemporary and perhaps there would be added benefits having the African contemporary tag thrown into the mix for good measure! The storming process continued, some of the questions we had to face from those such as the press and stakeholders were really about us trying to hold an identity that was void of imposed labels.

To some degree that continued for a long time. I really can't put my finger on the time or the place when we all began to sing from the same hymn sheet, however, we really did, and that's when I felt that the power of Phoenix voices starting to resonate. And to cut a rug through it, we could articulate what we wanted, that we were clear in our desires to be known as performers first and foremost. It wasn't appropriate to be called a troupe as some chose to do, we were a company. I don't believe there were any other companies doing what we were doing at that time, so little things became important to us. Other dance companies of our time were not being called 'troupes', so why Phoenix? The debates that were happening internally were resonating externally.

My personal journey within all of that continues, the support that I felt as an artist in the early stages of my career was developing, was coming through and not just in my physical contributions but the platform provided enabled me to stand up and be part of the backbone of the organisation. This was a gift. I recognise that now. Little did I know moving forward, this was beginning to position me in the sector. The platforms allowed me to have a voice that was authentic, to have a voice that I knew and could recognise, a voice that identified with the mission and a place for where I wanted to be.

JOINING PHOENIX AS ARTISTIC DIRECTOR

Here I'm going to jump forward considerably to when I became artistic director of Phoenix in 2009. My first programme was with Alesandra Seutin, Darshan Singh Bhuller, former artistic director of Phoenix, Douglas Thorpe, also a former Phoenix dancer, and a choreographer working out in the field, very niche in the way that he works, and myself. It is quite interesting that this programme was not recognised in the same way programmes are being recognised today! In spite of this I was very proud of that programme, it supported artists both male and female, and I know that for this publication we are specifically talking about females, however, the diverse make-up was a statement that unfortunately went under the radar. We've since continued to develop and help artists to launch their own careers in dance. As I've mentioned Douglas Thorpe, Kwesi Johnson, Bawren Tavaziva, Colin Poole, Robert Hylton, Warren Adams, a lot of successful males.

A lot of male voices working through the organisation, but the females, Alesandra and myself in terms of Black female choreographers, are few. Where are the female choreographers? More so, where are the Black female choreographers? And how do I as an artistic director continue to support and develop that? The females, however, in terms of their direction have gone on to influence and shape contemporary dance; Pam Johnson, Dawn Holgate, Jeanette Brookes, Godiva Marshall, all of whom have gone into positions of leadership in various forms, but we hear very little about them. We hear very little about the arguments that we were seeped in whilst building our careers. The male female balance is to be questioned. I am one of seven artistic directors of Phoenix Dance, five of us are BAME. Nevertheless, I feel there is an imbalance of how I am positioned within the sector, once again I ask the question of "what do we choose to see and what do we choose to acknowledge?"

Over the last 35 years Phoenix has a clear history that demonstrates the support of BAME artists, but it's this support that actually raises questions, and the questions come from externals asking what it is we are doing and what we are trying to achieve? We are supporting artists. When we have these conversations around artists, and discussing who they are and what they do, I tend to find that I'm also having to defend the fact that these artists very often do not always wish to be categorised in a way that puts them in a box and restricts their outward facing ability to have the freedom to be who they want to be and what kind of artist they can become. I started by saying, I don't make work that represents Blackness. I value the freedom of choice, to use whatever vocabulary serves the work most appropriately. Choreographers present to me on numerous occasions, feeling passionately that Phoenix is the platform where they can present their Blackness, in which they can present their arguments for the plight. I question how much I embrace in order to ensure that I am continuing to do and respect our mission. I'm convinced that art is there to open up thinking (as well as being entertaining). Phoenix enables artists to take that step closer to the work they choose to present. We are not a convenient mantle for others to pin their statements upon. It's not about representing slavery through Phoenix, it's not about representing conflict because of its Black identity and as a 'label' becoming a passport for others to take forward. I've since continued to work and commission new, past and existing artists to help build a diverse programme. My first programme which consisted of the four artists previously mentioned, which included me, was not a statement programme about Blackness. It represented artists that were, and could, be positioned in the mainstream. It's a philosophy in terms of my development, and my understanding of developing others. The integrity that underpins the reasons and focus of the work are all significant components, giving me guidance and supporting my decision making.

I've taken to headhunting in terms of keeping Phoenix alive regarding its representation of BAME artists/performers. I know our heritage is integral to our future. It's significantly important we remember where our past sits and how for me as an artist it helps me move forward supporting the ideas and the identity that Phoenix has embraced in becoming a multicultural organisation and what that references when I talk about that in the bigger picture, on the bigger stage. Actually in terms of representation, I have struggled on numerous occasions to find a way of addressing that within the organisation, not to be tokenistic, but to find a way to make it fit in and amongst everything else that we are trying to achieve. We've moved from being a company where 100% of the performers are Black. It's of significant importance that we have representation within the company. If we don't start to reflect and see difference within the artists as performers and creatives, surely we are in a position of diluting even further what is already relatively watered down.

I have the challenge of trying to sift many scenarios within my leadership role, I continue to play my part and in the past likened my role to that of a chameleon. I've listened to some of the contributing speakers talk about the complexities of choice and how sometimes there is no easy answer. Often assumptions are made based on one's own desires and limited understanding of the organisation, the unprecedented position and challenges it faces.

The balance is really fine, by no means am I saying I have the right balance right now, however, the last 7 years of my journey has highlighted how important it is that it sits at the heart of the conversations. To forget it risks believing that it doesn't exist, but it does. So it's really important in trying to figure out how seamlessly one can transfer, collate information, make connections, identify and present the logic, the rationale behind keeping the mission visible. It's akin of what we choose to acknowledge, what we choose to see and how we choose to move forward.

USING MY DUALITY AS STRENGTH

I guess really the games we need to play and the games we choose to play is an open pitch to all of us. We sometimes feel that we must be categorised, or we choose to sit in one half of the playing field when actually the field is there for us all to extend our game, and what does that mean, how can I find a way that actually extends my role as a leader to be able to invite, to engage and to offer out what is considered different? What actually is ownership of something that isn't primarily making a Black statement, but more so a statement about the person's art irrespective of colour? Thirty-five years on and Phoenix has carried that responsibility to a greater degree. Now more than ever we want to open that up, to strive with confidence, make an explicit statement that isn't a tokenistic approach to making and showing change.

Some choreographers have readily made their statement and wear the Black label consciously, others have categorically said "no, it's not about being a Black artist it's about being an artist". I respect both decisions.

I'm not afraid to look back, but sometimes looking back isn't where the answers lie. The only way is to move forward with the right voices and the right kind of support, identifying this as an essential part of the process can be the thing that makes you feel vulnerable. Sometimes, using my own duality to build strength is something I often do. It's very easy to do!

There is rarely just the one decision that suits everyone but everyone can be affected by that one decision. A reminder to self is that we as people of colour have earned the right to our positions and as people of colour we do not need to pay for the privilege. I often feel very responsible for more than myself in this position and actually the fact that in some shape or form, I should not feel guilty that I have not done it all, whatever 'all' is. This should not be a punishment. We should not put ourselves at the bottom of the to-do list, because if you do put yourself there, it's quite easy for others to do that for you. You should feel no remorse about the decisions that you have tried to forge and move forward, provided it's done with integrity and in the best interests of the people within your organisation. I think my journey firstly as a dancer then moving on to becoming rehearsal and tour director and now as director has served me well to serve the company.

It sits well with me having had working experiences with all of all previous directors. Each reincarnation has added to Phoenix's varied pallet, adding to its unique history.

It's also using the various dichotomies we face daily and using them to give us strength on whatever scale we perceive that to be; sometimes the smallest achievements have added value and surplus qualities making it more meaningful. So I think it's an interesting place where I sit and what I'm questioning. I sit in this organisation that I love, I adore, because its history tells me where I've been, and visioning a future tells me I can go much further. This job isn't just about me and my journey, my personal journey. I've been gifted an opportunity to do something different, I've been gifted an opportunity to make a change and embrace change with those that have also contributed to this publication. Holding onto that mantle is so important.

A few further thoughts that I've added to, in terms of looking back at this journey and my earlier question of how we have chosen to acknowledge and see where we've been. Within Phoenix there is always a challenge that gives it its unique stamp. I think there are some people who expect it to do certain things, there are some people who want it to change. Some people who don't believe Phoenix has done what it could, and others who think it's amazing for a combination of reasons. All of these varied views on Phoenix are absolutely acceptable! One model does not fit all! However, as my shoulders get broader and my confidence grows within the role, I take on board the various views, ascertain what's relevant to me right now, and make use of valuable opinions. What I want to do and share with an organisation like Phoenix and beyond is to clearly inform all involved that there is no blueprint for how to deliver the job. There certainly isn't a leadership model that wraps the process of directing up in one statement. Undoubtedly, there is not one method enabling any one individual to embrace art and culture. I am absolutely delighted that Phoenix is still going, I'm undeniably thrilled that I returned to the company as the artistic director after having a long history as a performer and rehearsal and tour director for the company. I sit here as a Black female and ask genuinely how many people see my colour? See my colour in this role? How many people acknowledge the person at the helm of the organisation because of my colour, or in spite of it? Would I face similar challenges if I directed any other organisation considered non-black?

Going back to the question I said that we should keep in mind at the beginning of this paper – what is it that we see? Do we categorise ourselves because we feel comfortable with that or are we really able to break down those barriers and step beyond that to enjoy what we really want to share with the wider world as artists, as friends, as fellow makers, as fellow critics? Can we do that? Can we see the commonality between us and actually acknowledge success when we see it?

Sharon Watson. Photographer Richard Moran.

Jasmyn Fyffe. Photographer Rob Rogers.

BLACK WOMEN IN DANCE STEPPING OUT OF THE BARRIERS

CONTRIBUTORS BIOGRAPHIES

ADESOLA AKINLEYE

Adesola Akinleye is an artist-scholar. She began her career as a dancer with Dance Theatre of Harlem. She later established her own company DancingStrong, which creates dance around the UK, American East Coast, Caribbean and Canada. Her most recent dance work Untitled: Women's Work (Flint) was an international commission by the Center for the Education of Women. The project informed a book chapter 'Her life in movement: reflections on embodiment as a methodology' in Researching Embodied Sport: exploring movement cultures edited by Dr. Ian Wellard, Routledge. Light Steps, a new work for young audiences, premiered at the Turner Contemporary Museum, UK 2014 followed by a UK tour in 2016.

Adesola is a Fellow of the RSA. She holds a Doctor of Philosophy in dance: sociology of the body and embodiment from Canterbury Christ Church University, UK. She has a Master of Arts in Work-based learning: dance in education and the community from Middlesex University, UK. A guest teacher and choreographer in a number of institutions and companies in UK, Canada and USA, including Dance Theatre of Harlem Summer programme, she is a part-time Senior Lecturer at Middlesex University.

Her interest in dance as a language for communication of embodied experience has led her to the Public Pedagogy of community informed starting points for art performance creation. Her performance work has a strong conceptual strand, ranging from concert dance to site-specific to installation-based performance.

www.dancingstrong.com

DEBORAH BADDOO

Deborah trained at the University of Surrey and went on to gain an MA in Performance Arts at Middlesex University. In 2006 she became a Fellow of the RSA. In 2010 she was awarded a MBE in the Queen's Honour's List for services to dance. Deborah also holds a Certificate in Training and Development, a Diploma in Arts Management and is a qualified coach.

Following on from her early career as a Senior Lecturer in Dance at Hackney Community College, London, where she established the first nationally accredited full-time Dance Foundation Course, Deborah went on to work at the Cockpit Theatre as a Youth Arts Development Manager and then as a dance development worker and co-founder of Pyramid Arts Development, a springboard for many artists' careers. A choreographer and performer in her own right, in 2012 she co-choreographed part of the opening ceremony for the Sailing Olympics in Weymouth.

Deborah established State of Emergency in 1986, a performance and production company, delivering a national and international programme of activity; commissioning and producing tours and events, delivering talent development programmes for young people, acting as an advocate for artists, and organising an annual leadership training programme for Artistic Directors. A National Portfolio Organisation of Arts Council England, State of Emergency leads the National Strategic Alliance for Black dance and recently established the first Black Dance Archive in the UK, funded by the Heritage Lottery Fund.

www.stateofemergencyltd.com

PAWLET BROOKES

Pawlet is an accomplished and experienced senior manager and producer who has been at the heart of the development of Black arts centres, from Marketing Manager at the Nia Centre (Manchester) in the 90s to the Artistic Director of Peepul Centre (Leicester) and Chief Executive of Rich Mix (London). She has been the Arts Council assessor for a number of Black arts capital projects, such as Bernie Grant Arts Centre (London) and National Centre for Carnival Arts (Luton).

Pawlet is the Founder and Artistic Director of Serendipity, a diversity-led organisation that initiated and produces LDIF (Let's Dance International Frontiers) as an annual festival in Leicester since 2011, and also delivers each year a Black History Month programme for Leicester, as well as many other projects.

She has edited and published "Serious About Dance – Let's Talk" in 2005, "Hidden Movement: Contemporary Voices of Black British Dance" in 2013, "Creolizing Dance in a Global Age" in 2015 and "Blurring Boundaries: Urban Street meets Contemporary Dance" in 2016.

During her extensive career she has programmed, commissioned or been the producer for a wide range of international artists, directors and companies, as diverse as: Soweto Kinch, Nina Simone, Steven Berkoff, Scottish Ballet, Geraldine Connor, Ballet Black, Mahogany Arts, Daksha Sheth Dance, Henri Oguike, Phillip Herbert, Mica Paris, Flawless, Barbara Hulanicki, Arlene Phillips, Akala, Gil Scott Heron, Aswad, Kyle Abraham and L'Acadco.

Her consultancy work includes leadership training, partnership building, artistic assessment, business planning, fund-raising (private and public sectors and charitable trusts), marketing, audience development and cultural diversity, events management and international programming. She was a finalist for the 2009 National Regeneration and Renewals Award for Cultural Leadership and has been a speaker at a number of international conferences, including being the UK representative at a UNESCO conference in Stockholm.

Pawlet is an Associate Lecturer at Falmouth University and Serendipity is a Company in Residence at De Montfort University.

www.serendipity-uk.com

CONTRIBUTORS BIOGRAPHIES

HILARY S. CARTY

Hilary Carty is an experienced consultant, facilitator and coach specialising in leadership development, management and organisational change. Rooted within the arts and cultural industries, Hilary draws on her creative acumen and experience to craft bespoke interactions for an eclectic range of sectors and businesses.

Prior to working independently, Hilary was the Director of the Cultural Leadership Programme, a £22m government investment in excellence in leadership within the UK cultural and creative industries.

Hilary's career demonstrates a successful record of senior level management experience in the arts, cultural and creative industries including Director, London (Arts) at Arts Council England; Director, Culture and Education at London 2012; and Director of Dance for Arts Council England.

Hilary holds an MBA from the University of Westminster; is a qualified coach with the Chartered Institute of Personnel and Development; and a qualified Organisation Development Practitioner with the NTL Institute, UK. She is also a Visiting Professor at Kufstein University, Austria. In recognition of her contribution to the arts, culture and the development of work-based learning, Hilary has been awarded Honorary Doctorates from the University of Westminster, De Montfort and Middlesex Universities; and Honorary Fellowship of Goldsmith's University of London.

www.co-creatives.co.uk

CATHERINE DÉNÉCY

Catherine Dénécy was born in the French island of Guadeloupe in the Caribbean where she started her professional training. She moved to New York City in 2004 to enter the Ailey School as the recipient of The Oprah Winfrey Foundation Scholarship. In 2005 she joined Urban Bush Women as a permanent member of the company during five seasons. She had the pleasure to premiere and perform works of artistic director and choreographer Jawole Willa Jo Zollar in the USA, in Europe, in South America and West Africa and also worked with renowned choreographers such as Nora Chipaumire and Camille Brown. In 2008 and 2009 she travelled to Senegal with Urban Bush Women to collaborate with the choreographer Germaine Acogny and her company Jant-Bi on the creation of "Scales of Memory", which toured the USA and Europe and was presented at the Festival des Arts Nègres in Dakar, Senegal in 2010.

In 2010, Catherine was also awarded the Grand Prix de la Création artistique de Guadeloupe for her dance project with set designer Soylé; 'UnpeuBeaucoupAlafoliePasdutout', co-produced by L'Artchipel, scène nationale de Guadeloupe. In 2011, she founded the BLISS Company to support her work and research in Contemporary Caribbean Dance on the international scene. In the meantime, she continued working with Jawole Willa Jo Zollar and Nora Chipaumire on 'Visible' which premiered at Harlem Stage, NYC. Between 2012-2013 Catherine toured 'Unpeubeaucoupalafoliepasdutout' in Guadeloupe, Jamaica, Dominica, Saint Lucia, England and Cuba and later had her first season in Paris, at Le Tarmac, for the Festival Outre Mer Veille.

She made her acting debut in the short film 'Bat Fanm aw mode d'emploi' directed by Abel Bichara as part of a national campaign against domestic violence. In 2014, Catherine went to West Hollywood, to study at the Lee Strasberg Film and Theater Institute. Whilst there, she played Velma Kelly in Chicago, The Musical at the Marilyn Monroe Theater. She later made her first TV appearance as one of the leading characters in Villa Karayib a Canal +'s serial (international network). Her work 'Mi-Chaud Mi-Froid: un ne peut pas tout le monde' was commissioned by L'Artchipel, scène nationale de Guadeloupe, as part of its artistic project on political mythologies. It world premiered at L'Artchipel in May 2015 and began touring internationally in 2016, with it's European premiere at LDIF 2016 as a site specific commission. With this new project, Catherine explores and works on the relation between the dancer and the musician, or the body and the instrument. While doing so, she challenges the codes and develops a refreshing and exalted contemporary dance.

CONTRIBUTORS BIOGRAPHIES

PAM JOHNSON

Born in Leeds, Pam trained in dance first as a founding student of the Northern School of Contemporary Dance (NSCD) and then at the London School of Contemporary Dance. Following this she enjoyed approximately 10 years as a dancer, choreographer and teacher. She joined DV8 Physical Theatre in 1987.

In 1989 Pam joined Phoenix Dance Company (as it was then known) as it formally incorporated female dancers for the first time. On leaving Phoenix, after nearly a decade with the company, and after a time as a freelance choreographer and dance participation specialist, she joined Kokuma Dance Theatre as their Education Outreach Officer. She returned to Leeds in 1999 as the NSCD's community and education manager, leading the institution's Widening Participation and Community Engagement strategies.

In 2003 she commenced a somewhat nomadic period with Arts Council England – first as their North West Dance Officer, then as a Relationship Manager, Dance with Arts Council (Yorkshire), and is now a Senior Relationship Manager in the Arts Council's London office. Retaining a dance specialism, Pam's responsibilities now also include oversight of the London Combined Arts and Dance portfolios and the co-ordination of Arts Council's Strategic Partnerships – relationships with London local government in particular.

MERCY NABIRYE

Mercy Nabirye served as Director for the Association of Dance of the African Diaspora (ADAD) in 2011 and then from 2013-2016 when ADAD, Dance UK, National Dance Teachers Association and Youth Dance England merged to become One Dance UK. Mercy steered ADAD to deliver its mission to promote the practice and appreciation of dance rooted in the African Diaspora, raising profiles of artists and the art forms. She led its national and international programmes at key venues, including Bloom National Festival celebrating dance of the African Diaspora across the UK regions, Re:generations International conference, a UK academic and artistic conference focusing on perspectives of the art forms; and a professional development fellowship Trailblazers which tailors a mentorship programme for future leaders for the dance sector. Mercy continues her leadership role with One Dance UK as a consultant.

Mercy's previous leadership roles include work at Apples and Snakes, England's leading performance poetry organisation; Creative Partnerships Kent, a creative learning initiative for Arts Council England; Future Creative CIC a social enterprise providing creative learning. She also works as an arts management consultant internationally.

Mercy graduated in Performing Arts in Uganda, East Africa; Film and Video Production at The American College in London UK as well as CIMA CBA Business Accounting. Her artistic background is as performer, choreographer, producer and writer for stage and screen. She is a member of the International Association of Blacks in Dance (USA) and Arterial Works (Africa).

MAUREEN SALMON

Maureen is the Founder Director of Freshwaters Consultancy which offers fresh thinking, new ideas and approaches in helping individuals and organisations create sustainable futures. Her practice is collaborative in design, development and delivery of programmes and projects in leadership, entrepreneurship and organisational development.

Maureen works in an international arena and has collaborated with cultural organisations in Africa, Brazil, Caribbean, China, India and USA. Clients have included: Walters & Cohen Architects, H2Dance, ADAD, Museums Association, Arts Council England Cultural Leadership Programme, National Cultural Foundation Barbados.

Maureen is a coach and an accredited emotional intelligence assessor.

Maureen was awarded 'Women of the Year' in 2000 at the 'Millennium Festival of Women's Work', 'European Federation of Black Women Business Owners' Professional Award'. She was a finalist in the 'European Union Women of Achievement Awards' 2001.

Maureen works for the University of the Arts as a Course Leader for BA (Hons) Design Management and Cultures, London College of Communication and is an Associate Lecturer for the EMBA (Fashion) and MA Fashion Management at the London College of Fashion.

www.freshwatersconsultancy.co.uk

JESSICA WALKER

Jessica recently graduated with a BA First Class Honours in Contemporary Dance and Choreography from De Montfort University, Leicester, and is currently studying for her Master's in Dance Performance at Trinity Laban as part of their internationally touring Transitions company.

Jessica was recently commissioned to create a piece, Exit Eve, for Channel 4's Random Acts platform for national broadcasting, and her autobiographical work Tick the Box (Mixed/Other) was performed at this year's Let's Dance International Frontiers festival. She has also spoken at national dance events, including the Black Women In Dance: Stepping Out of the Barriers conference.

Her role as Dance Ambassador for One Dance UK sees her engaging in political advocacy for the dance industry with MPs and governors, as well as networking with other artists and industry professionals. Jessica's interest in African Caribbean dance styles has enabled her to create a new codified movement technique respective to her own Jamaican-German heritage and explore the roles and responsibilities of the Mixed-Race choreographer.

CONTRIBUTORS BIOGRAPHIES

SHARON WATSON

Sharon trained at the London School of Contemporary Dance and danced with Spiral and Extemporary Dance Theatre before joining Phoenix as a dancer from 1989-1997. Whilst there she worked with choreographers such as Michael Clarke, Donald Byrd, Bebe Miller, Darshan Singh Bhuller and Philip Taylor. Sharon choreographed Never Still and Shaded Limits for Phoenix as well as creating new works for Northern School of Contemporary Dance, National Youth Dance Company and Union Dance. In 1996 she choreographed a piece specially commissioned for the opening ceremony of the Royal Armouries in Leeds. In 1998 she formed her own company ABCD.

Returning to Phoenix in 2000 as the company's Rehearsal and Tour Director, Sharon toured extensively in the UK and USA for 6 years. In 2006 she embarked upon a fellowship with the Clore Leadership Programme for which her secondment took her to the Sage Gateshead where she delivered a Choreographers and Composers course. In 2008, Sharon created and delivered Dancing with Rhinos as part of the regional Cultural Olympiad for Yorkshire and forming part of the practice research for her forming part of the practice research for her Performance Works MA from Leeds Metropolitan University. She spent 8 months as Director of Learning and Access at Northern Ballet Theatre.

Sharon was appointed as the 7th Artistic Director of Phoenix Dance Theatre in May 2009. In 2010 she was named as one of the Cultural Leadership Programme's Women to Watch. Since returning to Phoenix Sharon has choreographed Fast Lane for the Ignite tour, Melt for the company's Reflected programme and re-worked Never Still into Never 2 Still. Repetition of Change, featured as part of the successful Particle Velocity programme.

In 2013 Sharon choreographed pieces for the BBC's adaptation of Susanna Clarke's novel Jonathan Strange and Mr Norrell, broadcast in 2015. In 2014 Sharon choreographed three major commissions – Ghost Peloton, an ambitious collaboration with Scottish Public Arts charity NVA, in partnership with Sustrans, for Yorkshire Festival 2014 Grand Départ of the Tour de France; Honour, a multimedia live performance by Quays Culture for the centenary of WW1; and a large scale performance for the RFL Challenge Cup Final at Wembley.

Sharon is a trustee of Matthew Bourne's New Adventures, The Place, West Yorkshire Playhouse, and an artistic advisor for Central School of Ballet and Leeds Inspired. She was recently appointed as independent chair of the steering committee, bidding for European Capital of Culture Leeds 2023.

www.phoenixdancetheatre.co.uk

JAWOLE WILLA JO ZOLLAR

Jawole Willa Jo Zollar is the founder/Visioning Partner of Urban Bush Women. From Kansas City, Missouri, Jawole Willa Jo Zollar trained with Joseph Stevenson, a student of the legendary Katherine Dunham. After earning her B.A. in dance from the University of Missouri at Kansas City, she received her M.F.A. in dance from Florida State University. In 1980 Jawole moved to New York City to study with Dianne McIntyre at Sounds in Motion.

In 1984, Jawole founded Urban Bush Women (UBW) as a performance ensemble dedicated to exploring the use of cultural expression as a catalyst for social change. In addition to 34 works for UBW, she has created works for Alvin Ailey American Dance Theater, Philadanco, University of Maryland, Virginia Commonwealth University and others; and with collaborators including Compagnie Jant-Bi from Senegal and Nora Chipaumire. In 2006 Jawole received a New York Dance and Performance Award (Bessie) for her work as choreographer/creator of Walking With Pearl…Southern Diaries. Featured in the PBS documentary, Free to Dance, which chronicles the African-American influence on modern dance, Jawole was designated a Master of Choreography by the John F. Kennedy Performing Arts Center in 2005. Her company has toured five continents and has performed at venues including Brooklyn Academy of Music, Lincoln Center for the Performing Arts and The Kennedy Center. UBW was selected as one of three U.S. dance companies to inaugurate a cultural diplomacy programme for the U.S. Department of State in 2010. In 2011 Jawole choreographed Visible with Chipaumire, a theatrical dance piece that explores immigration and migration.

In 2012 Jawole was a featured artist in the film Restaging Shelter, produced and directed by Bruce Berryhill and Martha Curtis, and currently available to PBS stations.

Jawole developed a unique approach to enable artists to strengthen effective involvement in cultural organising and civic engagement, which evolved into UBW's acclaimed Summer Leadership Institute. She serves as director of the Institute, founder/visioning partner of UBW and currently holds the position of the Nancy Smith Fichter Professor of Dance and Robert O. Lawton Distinguished Professor at Florida State University.

A former board member of Dance/USA, Jawole received a 2008 United States Artists Wynn fellowship and a 2009 fellowship from the John Simon Guggenheim Memorial. Still dancing, she recently toured in a sold-out national tour presented by 651 ARTS as a leading influential dancer/choreographer on a programme that included her early mentor Dianne McIntyre, her collaborator Germaine Acogny, Carmen de Lavallade and Bebe Miller. As an artist whose work is geared towards building equity and diversity in the arts Jawole was awarded the 2013 Arthur L. Johnson Memorial award by Sphinx Music at their inaugural conference on diversity in the arts. In 2013, Jawole received the Doris Duke Performing Artist Award and recently received honorary degrees from Tufts University and Rutgers University. Recently, Jawole received the 2016 Dance Magazine award and the 2016 Dance/USA Honor Award.

www.urbanbushwomen.org